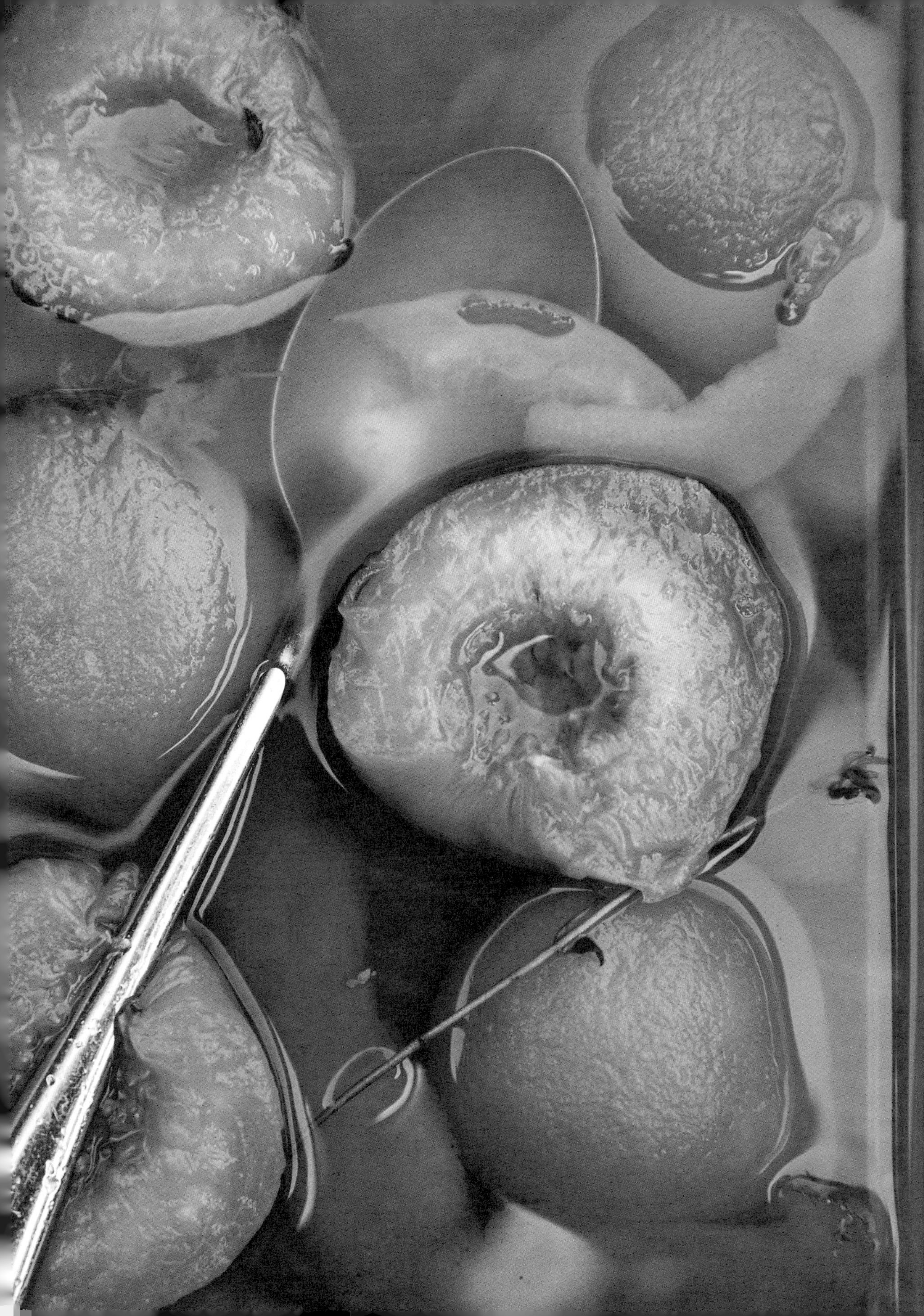

I'll Bring Dessert

Simple, Sweet Recipes for Every Occasion

Photography by Laura Edwards

Benjamina Ebuehi

Hardie Grant
QUADRILLE

RECIPE NOTES

Ingredients are listed using British terms and metric measurements first, followed by US terms and imperial/cup measurements in brackets. Please follow one system of measurement when following the recipes.

All eggs used are large and given in UK sizes. Readers in the US should go up a size. All milk used is full-fat.

introduction

Dessert is the best part of a meal. A strong statement, I know. I can already hear plenty of people disagreeing, but hear me out. For as long as I can remember, I've always felt the need for something sweet after eating. Like clockwork, after the last bite of lunch or dinner, my lips would pucker up in search of a little something to settle my sweet tooth. It could be as small as a square of chocolate, a digestive biscuit, or in times of desperation when cupboards were bare, a sweet milky cup of Horlicks. Just a little something to round things off.

It's the anticipation of dessert that I find particularly exciting. The plates are being cleared, there's still a bit of wine in your glass, the tablecloth stained with oily fingerprints and spillages, the conversations are deep and unreserved. Dessert is the feeling of knowing the night isn't quite over. It lets you linger that little bit longer. It's the signal to put the kettle on, to maybe move from the table to the comfy sofas. It's the joy of bringing a dish to the table and watching everyone's eyes light up, especially those who declared they didn't have any room but have since found the space.

I'm typically the designated dessert person. The one who volunteers (or is volunteered) to bring along something sweet, and it's a role I love and take very seriously. The person bringing dessert has much to consider. There are always a few questions that immediately come to mind:

- What's the vibe?
- Super casual or a bit more fancy?
- Do I go for a crowd pleaser or try something new?
- How much can I make in advance?
- Do I go hot or cold?
- Rich and creamy or something fruity?
- Will there be any vegans?
- What can I do that's maximum flavour but minimum effort?
- Should I just buy something?

So. Many. Questions. For some, it can be a little overwhelming and when I don't have the brain space to think, it's easy for me to resort to the same two or three favourites that stay in heavy rotation. Usually a tiramisu, cheesecake or pavlova. Don't get me wrong, these are all well-loved classics that are guaranteed to go down well (I've included three cheesecake recipes for you!) but sometimes you just want to mix things up. And I want this book to do the thinking for you! So if you're also the designated dessert person or you're bringing dessert for the very first time, this book will give you the answers and inspiration for what to make, no matter the occasion, and get you excited about all the sweet possibilities.

I'll Bring Dessert isn't a book full of restaurant-style, stuffy, plated desserts with tonnes of components and advanced techniques. Far from it. These are the recipes I make for cosy dinner parties with friends, for church potlucks, for those last-minute get-togethers, weekend lunches, big family Christmases and everything in between. The chapters are split based on how I initially approach what I want to make, but there's something for all seasons and moods in each chapter. I've included some vegan and gluten-free options and there are plenty of recipes that with a few easy swaps can be made dietary friendly. Some recipes come together in under an hour, and others are great for when you've got a bit more time to play with. I've only included recipes that transport well, either as a whole or as elements to be assembled later.

This book is a fun way to add some new desserts to your repertoire, and I've enjoyed bringing in my signature style of using lots of fresh herbs, spices and interesting ingredients, playing about with flavour in a relaxed and approachable way. Dessert is so joyful, it makes me smile just thinking about it, and it's even better when you get to make it and share with others. A little cheesy, I know, but still true.

I'm a dessert person through and through and always will be. I hope you become one too. Or at least after reading this book you're inspired to try something new and have the confidence to say 'I'll Bring Dessert'.

NOTES ON BRINGING DESSERT

So, you've decided what you're going to make, you've spent some time in the kitchen getting it ready and now the next step is getting it where it needs to be in one piece. These notes should help to make the whole process a bit easier.

Get organized: There's nothing worse than getting halfway through a recipe and realizing you don't have enough eggs or that something needs to be chilled overnight... but you need it today. Take a bit of time to read through the whole recipe and get familiar with the steps. Speaking from experience, you'll save yourself a lot of headache and potential tears if you do.

Making ahead: If you're bringing dessert, chances are you won't often have all day to spend in the kitchen getting things together. Many, if not the majority, of the desserts in this book can be made at least one day ahead, giving you time to spread things out and avoid last-minute panics. There'll be parts of some desserts that can be finished at your destination, like whipping fresh cream or adding final flourishes. But anything that needs quite a long time to chill, set or bake should ideally be done beforehand. In other words, don't rock up and start rolling out the pastry for your pie.

Reheating: If something requires reheating, I'll often leave it in the pan or dish it was baked in for ease, cover with foil and just pop it in the oven towards the end of dinner so it's ready to go.

If I'm bringing something that's assembled but not cooked yet, like a crumble, then I put this on a little earlier and set a timer so I don't forget and get lost in all the good conversations. (This has definitely happened to me.)

Heating up a whole cake rather than slices is usually better as it stops exposed edges from getting too crisp.

Remember not to have the oven temperature too high – you're just reheating not continuing the cooking process, so around 150°C (130°C fan/ 300°F/gas mark 2) should be fine. Some desserts are happy to have a quick blast in the microwave for a few seconds, and if time is of the essence, then go for it.

Tupperware: Investing in some larger-sized airtight tupperware will come in handy. I have a couple that are big enough to fit a 23-cm (9-in) cake or 33 x 23-cm (13 x 9-in) traybake. Having these to hand will minimize any panic of finding something to put your dessert in at the last minute. I usually line them with a sheet of baking paper and this helps lift things out.

Cake boxes: These disposable boxes are great for more than just cake and I'll use them for cookies, pies and tarts and anything that's a bit oddly shaped or too tall for my tupperware. And they get bonus points because you don't have to worry about remembering to get it back at the end of the night.

Essentials: If you're new to the dessert crew and want to invest in some key equipment, I'd say the following is a good place to start:

- A loose bottomed 20-cm (8-in) cake pan: the majority of the cakes in this book are baked in this tin.

- A 20- or 23-cm (8- or 9-in) fluted tart pan.

- A ceramic or glass dish for desserts like tiramisu and other baked puddings.

- An electric whisk: it doesn't need to be a super-expensive one, but it will save a lot of time and energy in the kitchen.

- Oven thermometer: there are many reasons why a bake might fail, but a likely culprit is your oven. Every home oven behaves differently so placing a free-standing thermometer inside is a big help and much more reliable at telling you what the temperature actually is. The first time I got one, I was surprised to see my oven running nearly 20°C cooler than the dial displayed.

Custard: An absolute staple when it comes to serving dessert. As much as I love making custard, I appreciate that not everyone wants to, nor has the time to, make it from scratch, and there are times when only shop-bought custard will do. Whether that's the Madagascan vanilla-specked tubs from M&S or a good carton of Ambrosia, choose your favourite and bring it along.

Ice cream: I treat ice cream a bit differently to custard and will always go for shop-bought. I bought an ice-cream attachment for my stand mixer years ago and had every intention of being that person who'd churn out a new flavour every week. It got used once. If you love making ice cream, then by all means continue! But there are an incredible number of good-quality options and flavours out there, so just choose something that suits your budget and pick it up on the way to your destination.

quick picks

For the times when you're feeling a bit indecisive or when you know what the vibe is but are still a bit unsure of what to choose, I've put together this list to give you some quick inspiration.

Something that feels fancy:
Salted honey sesame tart

Something speedy:
Last-minute strawberries & cream

Something classic:
Tiramisu

Something that looks like you made a lot of effort but didn't:
Burnt Basque cheesecake

Something that is actually a lot of effort but worth it:
Pistachio gâteau Basque

Something for a crowd:
Chocolate buttermilk traybake with muscovado frosting & thyme caramel

Something for the vegans:
Creamy coconut & passionfruit tart

Something for summer:
Hot honey peach shortcakes

Something boozy:
Irish cream chocolate mousse

Something festive:
Gingerbread roulade

Something your mum would love:
My perfect crumble

Something casual:
Halva & smoked salt chocolate cookies

something fruity

Fruit desserts are timeless. As the seasons come and go, there's something new to play around with and incorporate into something sweet to end a meal. With fruit, a lot of the time, less is more. A simple poached peach can stay on your mind for weeks afterwards and macerated strawberries in the height of summer fill me with joy. I use a mix of fresh, frozen and tinned fruit throughout the chapter to give more flexibility, but feel free to play around and mix and match to suit what you have.

cherry slab pie

MAKE AHEAD

Make up to 1 day ahead.

If you're bringing a dessert for a crowd, consider making this slab pie. Made in one large tray, it feeds plenty and is ideal for those who aren't keen on the lower crust-to-fruit ratio you get in deeper filled pies. Plus, you get corner pieces! This is one you can make all year round by using frozen cherries, which I often do. A little lemon and balsamic vinegar brings enough acidity to make the cherries sing as they bubble away in the crust. I always bring this in the pan it was baked in; it makes it super-easy to pop back in the oven to reheat.

Serves 12–16

For the pastry

250g (9oz/1 cup plus 2 Tbsp) cold unsalted butter, diced, plus extra for greasing
430g (15oz/3¼ cups) plain (all-purpose) flour, plus extra for dusting
½ tsp fine sea salt
45g (1½oz/¼ cup) caster (superfine) sugar
60–90ml (2–2½fl oz/4–6 Tbsp) cold water

For the filling

1kg (2lb 3oz) pitted cherries (fresh or frozen)
130g (4¾oz/⅔ cup) caster (superfine) sugar
15g (½oz/1½ Tbsp) cornflour (cornstarch)
juice of ½ lemon
2 tsp balsamic vinegar

To finish

1 egg, beaten
demerara (turbinado) sugar

To make the pastry, add all the ingredients except the water to a bowl and give it a quick mix to coat the butter in the flour. Use your fingertips to rub the butter into the flour until you have a coarse mixture with some pieces of butter a little larger than peas.

Make a well in the centre and add in 60ml (4 Tbsp) water. Use a table knife to stir to get a shaggy dough. If the dough still looks really dry, keep adding water a tablespoon at a time. You don't want a sticky dough, so be careful not to add too much. Turn the dough out onto a very lightly floured surface and use your hands to bring it together into a thick, rough rectangle. Wrap in plastic wrap and chill in the fridge for 2–3 hours or until firm.

Lightly grease a 33- x 23-cm (13- x 9-in) sheet pan (or you can use a baking tray with sides about 2.5cm (1in) high.

Once chilled, split your dough into 2 pieces, with one portion being a little bigger than the other (about a 60/40 split). Lightly dust your work surface and roll out the bigger piece about 4cm (1½in) bigger than your pan. Line your pan with the pastry, making sure to press it into the edges and leaving an overhang of pastry around the rim.

If you're using frozen cherries, make sure to thaw completely and get rid of two-thirds of any liquid that's released. Add all the ingredients for the cherries to a bowl and mix to combine. Fill the pastry-lined pan with the cherries and any of the liquids left behind. Roll out the second piece of dough and carefully lay it on top of the cherries. Pinch the edges of the top and bottom crust together to seal and use your fingers to crimp.

Chill in the fridge for 30 minutes (or the freezer for 15 if you have space).

Preheat the oven to 210°C (190°C fan/ 410°F/gas mark 7) and place a large baking sheet inside to heat up too.

Brush the surface of the pie with the beaten egg and sprinkle generously with demerara sugar. Make 4 small slits in the centre of the pie to let steam escape and place it directly on the hot baking sheet in the oven (this will help to evenly cook the base).

Bake for 20 minutes before lowering the oven temperature to 190°C (170°C fan/ 375°F/gas mark 5) and baking for 45–50 minutes until the pie is deeply golden and the cherry juices are bubbling.

Remove from the oven and let it cool for 30 minutes before slicing and serving.

hot honey peach shortcakes

Shortcakes are for summer. Well, you can have them whenever you want, but when filled with juicy stone fruit and clouds of cream it just transports me to warm, breezy, care-free afternoons. The buttery shortcakes are filled with plump peaches soaked in hot honey, and cream that has been whipped just enough to hold its shape. This is very much a make-your-own sort of dessert; add all the bits to the table and let everyone put it together.

Serves 6

150g (5½oz/generous ½ cup) honey
1–2 tsp dried chilli (red pepper) flakes
1 tsp lemon juice
3 ripe peaches, pitted and each cut into 8
300ml (10½fl oz/generous 1¼ cups) double (heavy) cream

For the shortcakes

275g (9¾oz/2 cups) plain (all-purpose) flour
50g (1¾oz/⅓ cup) fine cornmeal (polenta)
50g (1¾oz/¼ cup) caster (superfine) sugar
3 tsp baking powder
¼ tsp fine sea salt
160g (5¾oz/scant ¾ cup) cold unsalted butter, diced
200g (7oz/scant 1 cup) buttermilk
a little milk, for brushing
demerara (turbinado) sugar, for sprinkling

For the shortcake, add the flour, cornmeal, sugar, baking powder and salt to a large bowl and mix to combine. Add in the diced butter and use your fingertips to rub it into the flour. You want the mixture to be quite coarse, with most of the butter the size of peas and a few chunks a bit larger.

Make a well in the centre and pour in the buttermilk. Gently stir until you have a rough, shaggy dough. Turn it out onto a lightly floured surface and gently pat it into a rectangle about 2.5cm (1in) thick. Using a sharp knife or bench scraper, slice the dough into 4 and stack the pieces up on top of each other. Use your hands to flatten the stack back down into a rectangle, tidying up the edges with the back of a knife. (This method helps to give flaky layers.)

Slice into 6 pieces and place them on a large baking tray lined with baking paper. Chill in the freezer for 15 minutes or in the fridge for 30 minutes.

Preheat the oven to 200°C (180°C fan/400°F/gas mark 6).

Brush the tops with a little milk and sprinkle some demerara sugar on top. Bake for 24–27 minutes or until golden and the bases sound hollow when tapped. Let them cool completely on a wire rack.

To make the filling, add the honey and chilli to a shallow saucepan. Let it simmer for 1–2 minutes before stirring in the lemon juice. Toss in the peaches and let it simmer for another minute before removing from the heat and setting aside to cool.

Lightly whip the cream and chill in the fridge until needed.

When you're ready to serve, you can place everything in dishes on the table for people to assemble themselves. Slice the shortcakes in half and drizzle some of the honey on each side before topping with some cream and peach slices.

MAKE AHEAD

Make the shortcakes a day ahead and freshen them up for 5–7 minutes in a warm oven.

white-wine-poached peaches with wholemeal shortbread

MAKE AHEAD

Make the peaches up to 2 days ahead and store in the fridge with the poaching liquid. The shortbread can be made up to 2 days ahead.

If in doubt, poach some fruit. There is such a quiet beauty in delicately poached fruit, soft enough to give way to your spoon but firm enough to hold its shape. Peaches are one of my favourites to poach – the colour alone is so pleasing and, when served cold, makes for the most refreshing summery dessert. They are perfect for making ahead; as the peaches sit in the syrup, they'll soak up even more flavour. My ideal way to eat them is with a good drizzle of cold cream or sitting in a lake of crème anglaise (page 176).

I'm not a wine expert by any means, so use a wine that you like to drink. Something on the drier side tends to work really well.

Serves 4

450ml (15¼fl oz/scant 2 cups) white wine
200g (7oz/1 cup) caster (superfine) sugar
pared zest (using a swivel peeler) of 1 lemon
3 sprigs of thyme
4 ripe peaches, halved and pitted

For the shortbread

100g (3½oz/scant ½ cup) salted butter
40g (1½oz/3¼ Tbsp) caster (superfine) sugar, plus extra to finish
130g (4½oz/1 cup) wholemeal (wholewheat) flour
½ Tbsp cornflour (cornstarch)

Add the wine, sugar, zest and thyme to a large saucepan. Heat until the sugar dissolves and then add the peach halves, cut side down. Poach the peaches gently for 5 minutes before flipping them over and poaching for another 2–3 minutes. If your peaches are really firm, they'll take a bit longer. You're looking for them to be softened enough for a knife to pierce through but still holding their shape.

Turn off the heat, scoop the peaches out of the liquid and place them cut side down on a plate. When cool enough to handle, remove the skins – they should peel off quite easily. If you're making these ahead of time, let the poaching liquid cool and pour it into an airtight container, placing the peaches back inside. Store in the fridge until needed.

To make the shortbread, preheat the oven to 190°C (170°C fan/375°F/gas mark 5). Line a small lipped baking tray with baking paper.

Cream the butter and sugar together for 1–2 minutes – we don't need it to be super fluffy, just well combined. Tip in the flour and cornflour and stir until you get a thick dough.

Pat the dough into the lined tray, flattening it as much as you can. Use a knife to score the shortbread into fingers (don't cut all the way through) and prick each biscuit with a fork.

Bake for 20–25 minutes until the shortbread is lightly browned. Sprinkle generously with sugar before slicing into fingers, using the scored lines to guide you. Let them cool completely before serving alongside the peaches, some cold cream and some of the poaching liquid.

tarragon plum cobbler

MAKE AHEAD

Make up to 1 day ahead and reheat in the oven to serve.

I've yet to meet anyone who doesn't like a cobbler. Warm, jammy fruits and a knobbly buttery top, it's an ideal all-year-round sort-of pudding that can be thrown together fairly quickly without too much forward planning.

Herbs and fruits will always be my jam, and tarragon is a quiet player that brings just enough aniseed/liquorice vibes that still works for people, like myself, who don't like liquorice.

Best served warm from the oven while the juices still have a little movement, this is one I like to prep beforehand and pop into the oven while we're still on savoury.

Serves 6–8

For the plums

80g (2¾oz/scant ⅔ cup) caster (superfine) sugar (you may need a touch more if your plums are quite tart, so taste and adjust)
7 sprigs of fresh tarragon
10 small plums (or 8 bigger), pitted and quartered
2 Tbsp water
½ tsp vanilla bean paste

For the cobbler

75g (2½oz/½ cup plus 1 Tbsp) plain (all-purpose) flour
75g (2½oz/½ cup plus 1 Tbsp) spelt flour (or you can use all plain if preferred)
30g (1oz/2½ Tbsp) caster sugar
60g (2¼oz/¼ cup) cold salted butter, diced
100ml (3½fl oz/scant ½ cup) double (heavy) cream

Preheat the oven to 190°C (170°C fan/ 375°F/gas mark 5).

Add the sugar and tarragon to a food processor and blitz briefly to break down the tarragon.

Add the plum quarters and vanilla to a baking dish and spoon the tarragon sugar on top. Give it all a good mix so the plums are coated, then drizzle the water on top. Cover loosely with foil and bake in the oven for 20 minutes until the plums have started to soften and release some of their juices. Remove from the oven and set aside to cool a little. Let cool completely if you're making in advance.

To make the cobbler, add the flours and sugar to a bowl and mix to combine. Toss in the butter and use your fingertips to rub it into the flour. Make a well in the centre and pour in the cream. Give it a stir to combine until you have a rough, soft dough. It doesn't need to be smooth, so be careful not to overwork it.

Using a tablespoon, add dollops of the cobbler on top of the plums, leaving some of the fruit poking through. Bake for 30–35 minutes until the cobbler is golden and the fruit juices are bubbling underneath.

Serve the cobbler warm with ice cream or cold cream.

apple olive oil cake

This is a warming, lightly spiced apple cake that is exactly what you want on a cosy autumn afternoon or evening. Upside down cakes aren't typically my thing, but this I'll make an exception for. It reheats really well, so serve it warm when the topping is still sticky and moist, and pour over some cold cream. And it's a perfect one to make plant-based – simply swap out the butter in the topping for something dairy-free.

Serves 8

75g (5 Tbsp) olive oil, plus extra for greasing
175g (6oz/1⅓ cups) plain (all-purpose) flour
140g (5oz/¾ cup minus 2 tsp) light brown sugar
2 tsp ground cinnamon
2 tsp baking powder
½ tsp fine sea salt
150ml (5fl oz/scant ⅔ cup) oat milk
1 tsp vanilla bean paste
2 tsp apple cider vinegar

For the topping
40g (1½oz/3 Tbsp) unsalted butter
70g (2½oz/generous ⅓ cup) light brown sugar
¼ tsp fine sea salt
2 eating apples (I use Braeburn or Cox)

Preheat the oven to 180°C (160°C fan/350°F/gas mark 4). Grease a 20-cm (8-in) round springform cake pan and line the base with baking paper.

For the topping, add the butter, sugar and salt to a small saucepan and heat gently until heated. Bring to the boil and let it simmer for a minute, then carefully pour into the prepared cake pan.

Core your apples and slice in half. Thinly slice each half into half-moons, cutting as evenly as possible and then, starting from the middle, arrange them in the cake pan on top of the caramel, letting them overlap a little. Set aside while you make the batter.

Add the flour, sugar, cinnamon, baking powder and salt to a bowl and mix to combine.

In a jug (pitcher), mix together the oil, oat milk, vanilla and apple cider vinegar.

Make a well in the centre of your dry ingredients and pour in the liquids. Give it a gentle mix until you have a smooth batter.

Pour this on top of the apples and smooth the top. Place the cake pan on a baking tray to catch any leakage and bake for 45–55 minutes, until the cake feels springy to the touch and a skewer inserted into the centre comes out clean.

Let the cake cool for 5 minutes before placing your serving plate on top. Flip the cake over and carefully remove the pan. Serve warm or at room temperature, with cream.

To transport this, keep it in the pan and reheat in the oven for 10 minutes until the bottom is hot, before flipping.

MAKE AHEAD

Best made on the day.

rhubarb meringue cake

There are a few elements that make up this cake, but it's so worth it. It's all about the different textures here – soft, squidgy sponge, marshmallowy meringue with crisp edges, silky folds of cream and tender, hot pink rhubarb roasted just enough to keep its bite. If you can't get hold of rhubarb, this cake still works with a range of fruit. Try it with the sumac strawberries on page 126, the white-wine poached peaches on page 22, or keep it super-simple with a mix of fresh berries.

Serves 12–16

For the rhubarb

300g (10½oz) rhubarb
3 Tbsp caster (superfine) sugar
grated zest of 1 lemon
2 Tbsp water

For the cake

125g (4½oz/½ cup plus 1 Tbsp) unsalted butter
150g (5½oz/¾ cup) caster (superfine) sugar
½ tsp vanilla bean paste
1 egg, plus 2 egg yolks
grated zest of 1 lemon
175g (6oz/1⅓ cups) plain (all-purpose) flour
1½ tsp baking powder
pinch of fine sea salt
100ml (3½fl oz/scant ½ cup) milk

Start by making the rhubarb. Preheat the oven to 210°C (190°C fan/410°F/gas mark 6).

Wash your rhubarb and trim off the ends. Chop into 5-cm (2-in) pieces and place in a roasting dish. Toss with the sugar, lemon zest and water. Cover loosely with foil and roast in the oven for 12–15 minutes until the rhubarb has softened a little but is still holding its shape. Baste the rhubarb in some of the juices and set aside to cool completely. (You can do this step a few days in advance and store the rhubarb in the fridge.)

Turn the oven down to 180°C (160°C fan/350°F/gas mark 4). Grease a 33- x 23-cm (13- x 9-in) Swiss roll (jelly roll) pan or baking tray at least 2cm (¾in) deep and line it with baking paper, leaving enough overhang to help you pull it out later.

Add the butter, sugar and vanilla to a bowl and cream together with an electric whisk or stand mixer until pale and creamy.

Add in the egg yolks one at a time, beating well after adding, and then beat in the whole egg, scraping down the sides of the bowl often. Add in half of the flour, the baking powder and salt, stirring to get a smooth batter. Mix in the milk followed by the rest of the flour.

MAKE AHEAD

Make the rhubarb up to 3 days ahead and store in the fridge. The cake can be made a day before but I find it's best on the day it was made.

continued overleaf

rhubarb meringue cake continued

For the meringue

120g (4¼oz) egg whites (from 3 large eggs)
170g (6oz/generous ¾ cup) caster (superfine) sugar
1 tsp cornflour (cornstarch)

To finish

400ml (14fl oz/1¾ cups) double (heavy) cream (or use three-quarters cream and a quarter custard)
1 tsp vanilla bean paste

Spoon the batter into the lined pan and smooth out the top. Bake for 20–25 minutes or until the cake is lightly browned and cooked through.

While the cake bakes, prepare the meringue. Add the egg whites to a clean, grease-free bowl and whip on medium speed until they look frothy and have soft peaks. Start adding in the sugar a tablespoon at a time, waiting about 20 seconds before adding more. Once all the sugar is in, tip in the cornflour and whisk briefly to combine.

Spoon the meringue onto the cake once it comes out of the oven, using a palette knife or the back of a spoon to create swoops and swirls. Place it back in the oven and turn the temperature up to 190°C (170°C fan/375°F/gas mark 5).

Bake for another 20–25 minutes or until the meringue has a firm outer crust and is starting to lightly brown. Remove from the oven and set aside to cool completely.

When you're ready to serve, lightly whip the cream and vanilla in a bowl until you have soft peaks (stirring in the custard, if using). Spoon the cream on top of the meringue and top with the rhubarb and some of the syrup.

lemon & berry summer cake

This is a proper big, fat summer cake with all the best things. A soft, lemony sponge that's super-easy to make (no mixer required), layered up with creamy mascarpone and lots of fresh berries. This is for the summer parties and the family BBQs where you want to go big.

Serves 12

For the sponge

200g (7oz/¾ cup plus 2 Tbsp) unsalted butter, melted, plus extra for greasing
360g (12¾oz/2¾ cups) plain (all-purpose) flour
360g (12¾oz/1¾ cups) caster (superfine) sugar
1 Tbsp plus 1 tsp baking powder
¼ tsp fine sea salt
5 eggs
200ml (7fl oz/scant 1 cup) milk
100g (3½oz/scant ½ cup) neutral oil (such as sunflower or vegetable)
grated zest of 2 lemons
1½ tsp vanilla bean paste

For the syrup

100ml (3½fl oz/scant ½ cup) lemon juice
120g (4¼oz/scant ⅔ cup) caster (superfine) sugar

Preheat the oven to 180°C (160°C fan/350°F/gas mark 4). Grease three 20-cm (8-in) round cake pans and line with baking paper.

Add the flour, sugar, baking powder and salt to a large bowl and mix to combine.

In a jug (pitcher), mix together the eggs, milk, oil, lemon zest and vanilla. Pour the wet ingredients into the dry and mix until you have a smooth batter. Stir in the melted butter.

Pour the batter into the prepared cake pans and bake for 20–25 minutes until nicely browned and a skewer inserted into the centre comes out clean.

While they bake, make the lemon syrup. Add the lemon juice and sugar to a small saucepan and bring to the boil. Let it simmer for 1–2 minutes and set aside to cool.

Prick holes across the surface of the cooked cakes and spoon the syrup evenly over each one. Let them cool completely and, if you're making them in advance, wrap well in plastic wrap.

MAKE AHEAD

Make the cake layers up to 2 days in advance and keep them well wrapped. Make the berries the day before and store in the fridge. The mascarpone filling should be made just before assembling.

continued overleaf

lemon & berry summer cake continued

For the compote

300g (10½oz) blackberries
200g (7oz) blueberries
150g (5½oz/¾ cup) caster (superfine) sugar
juice of ½ lemon
200g (7oz) raspberries, plus extra to serve

For the mascarpone filling

350g (12oz/generous 1½ cups) mascarpone
200g (7oz/scant 1½ cups) icing (confectioners') sugar
270g (9½oz/1¼ cups) cream cheese
1 tsp vanilla bean paste
200ml (7fl oz/scant 1 cup) double (heavy) cream

For the compote, add the blackberries and blueberries to a small pan with the sugar and lemon juice. Bring to a low boil and cook for 2–3 minutes until the berries are softened and syrupy. Stir through the raspberries and set aside to cool.

For the mascarpone filling, add the mascarpone and icing sugar to a bowl and use a whisk to beat until just smooth. Mix in the cream cheese and vanilla until you have no lumps, then use a spatula to gently fold in the cream. This filling is easy to overwhip so be careful!

To assemble, use a serrated knife to level the cakes if they are uneven. Place one cake on a cake stand or serving plate and spoon on just under a third of the mascarpone filling, spreading it out evenly with a palette knife. Top with some of the berry compote and place the next cake layer on top. Repeat the process with more mascarpone and berries and place the last cake layer topside down. Finish with the remaining mascarpone and some fresh raspberries.

preserved lemon olive oil cookies

MAKE AHEAD

Make up to 2 days ahead and store in an airtight container.

These soft, almost squidgy cookies are fragrant with lemon and come with a pleasant savouriness from the olive oil. If you're bringing dessert for people who don't have a massive sweet tooth, then these are a good option. They're what I make if I know we're having quite a heavy meal and we'll need something a bit lighter. Although I have to point out they double up exceedingly well as ice-cream sandwiches.

Makes 12

150g (5½oz/¾ cup) caster (superfine) sugar
60g (2¼oz/5 Tbsp) light brown sugar
100ml (3½fl oz/scant ½ cup) extra virgin olive oil
½ tsp vanilla bean paste
1 egg, plus 1 egg yolk
2 Tbsp preserved lemon peel, finely chopped
275g (9¾oz/2 cups) plain (all-purpose) flour
½ tsp bicarbonate of soda (baking soda)

Add both sugars, the oil and vanilla to a bowl and mix to combine. Stir in the egg and egg yolk, followed by the preserved lemon peel.

Add the flour and bicarbonate of soda and stir until you have a thick dough. Cover and chill in the fridge for 2 hours or until firm.

Preheat the oven to 200°C (180°C fan/ 400°F/gas mark 6). Line 2 baking trays with baking paper.

Roll the dough into 12 balls and spread them out across the two trays. Bake for 15–20 minutes until the edges are set and the middle is still a little soft.

Let them cool completely before serving.

spiced pineapple tart with bay cream

There are some items that you're almost guaranteed to find in most kitchen cupboards or pantries. Canned fruit is one of them. For me, it's usually pineapple or peaches and as much as canned fruit can get a bad rap, it comes in so handy for those last-minute 'not sure what to make for dessert' kind of moments. Use shop-bought pastry for an even quicker bake and then all that's left to do is assemble and stick it in the oven. The tart is best eaten on the day it's made but does reheat well in the oven. And please don't skip the bay cream! It cuts through some of the sweetness, with warming herbal notes.

Serves 9

- 1 x 320g (11¼oz) sheet of ready-rolled, all-butter puff pastry
- 1 egg, beaten
- 1 x 435g (15oz) can of sliced pineapple
- 50g (1¾oz/¼ cup) light brown sugar
- ¼ tsp fresh grated nutmeg
- ½ tsp ground cinnamon
- 50g (1¾oz/3½ Tbsp) salted butter, melted

For the bay cream

- 250ml (9fl oz/generous 1 cup) double (heavy) cream
- 1 tsp light brown sugar
- 5 fresh bay leaves

Unroll the puff pastry onto a baking tray. Starting from one of the shorter ends, trim off 4 strips of pastry about 1cm (½in) wide. You'll be left with one large square, and then the strips will make your frame.

Brush the edges of the square with a little beaten egg, and lay the strips of pastry on top. You may need to trim some of the ends off to get a neat square. Prick the inside of the pastry frame all over with a fork and then place in the fridge to chill while you prepare the filling and preheat the oven to 200°C (180°C fan/400°F/gas mark 6).

Drain the pineapples and discard (or drink!) the juice. In a small bowl, mix the sugar, nutmeg and cinnamon together.

Brush the pastry base with some of the melted butter and top with half of the sugar mixture. Arrange the slices of pineapple on top – you'll have to cut some slices in half or quarters to fill in gaps. Brush the tops of the pineapple with more melted butter and sprinkle the remaining sugar on top.

Brush the pastry frame with egg wash and bake for 30–35 minutes, until the pastry is well browned. Set aside to cool.

For the bay cream, add the cream, sugar and bay leaves to a small pan and heat gently to dissolve the sugar. Remove from the heat, cover and let the bay infuse for at least 15 minutes. You can serve the cream chilled or gently reheat to serve warm.

MAKE AHEAD

Best made on the day.

thyme-roasted grapes with whipped ricotta

MAKE AHEAD

You can whip the ricotta up to 2 days before and store in a sealed container in the fridge. The grapes are best made on the day you plan to serve.

Roasted grapes might sound a little strange, especially for a dessert, but trust me, it works. This leans more on the savoury side and is perfect for those who are more likely to choose the cheeseboard over the chocolate cake. I serve these with thinly sliced toasted ciabatta with a drizzle of olive oil and some crunchy demerara (turbinado), because more bread at the end of the meal should definitely be a thing.

Serves 6

500g (1lb 2oz) red grapes, ideally a mix of colours
5–6 sprigs fresh thyme
1½ Tbsp honey
1 Tbsp olive oil, plus extra to serve

For the whipped ricotta
250g (9oz/generous 1 cup) ricotta
150g (5½oz/ scant ⅔ cup) Greek yoghurt
grated zest of 1 lemon
½ tsp vanilla bean paste
1 Tbsp honey

To serve (optional)
toasted ciabatta or crusty bread
demerara (turbinado) sugar

Preheat the oven to 210°C (190°C fan/ 410°F/gas mark 6).

Add the grapes and thyme to a baking dish. Drizzle the honey and olive oil on top and toss to coat, or just get in with your fingers.

Roast for 15–20 minutes until the grapes start to blister and become softened and syrupy. Set them aside to cool.

Add all the ingredients for the whipped ricotta to a food processor and blitz until smooth and creamy.

Add the grapes and all the juices to a shallow dish and the ricotta to another. Serve with toasted ciabatta or crusty bread, drizzled with olive oil and sprinkled with demerara. Or for something sweeter, serve with tuiles (page 185).

hibiscus & buttermilk jelly

I went back and forth deciding whether to include a jelly (jello) recipe in this book. It's not something I make very often; I've got to be in a very specific mood for it but when the craving hits, this is what I'd go for.

My best jelly memories are as a child at school being served neon-red scoops that I'd shake vigorously, watching it nearly jiggle right off my plate. Served with the cheapest vanilla ice cream, it was such a treat. This version is a little more grown up, with a hibiscus jelly spiked with fresh ginger and orange, layered with milky buttermilk jelly.

Serves 6–8

For the hibiscus layer

7 gelatine leaves (platinum grade)
30g (1oz) dried hibiscus flowers
650ml (22fl oz/2¾ cups) water
90g (3¼oz/scant ½ cup) caster (superfine) sugar
20g (¾oz) fresh ginger, peeled and sliced
pared zest (using a swivel peeler) of 1 orange
1 cinnamon stick

For the buttermilk layer

2½ gelatine leaves (platinum grade)
250ml (9fl oz/generous 1 cup) buttermilk
70ml (2¼fl oz/4½ Tbsp) milk
40g (1½oz/3¼ Tbsp) caster (superfine) sugar
1 tsp vanilla bean paste

For the hibiscus layer, add the gelatine leaves to a small bowl of cold water and set aside.

Add the hibiscus, water, sugar, ginger, orange zest and cinnamon to a saucepan and bring to boil. Reduce the heat down to a simmer and let it gently bubble away for about 15 minutes. Remove from the heat and strain into a jug (pitcher).

Take the gelatine out of the water and squeeze to remove any excess water. Add the gelatine to the hibiscus and stir until dissolved. Pour it into a jelly mould and leave to cool to room temperature before chilling in the fridge for 2 hours.

To make the buttermilk layer, add the gelatine sheets to a bowl of cold water.

Add the buttermilk, milk, sugar and vanilla to a small saucepan and heat gently until the sugar has dissolved and the buttermilk is warmed through. Remove from the heat and let it cool a little. Add the gelatine leaves to the pan, stirring to dissolve. Let it cool for about 15 minutes before pouring on top of the hibiscus layer.

Chill in the fridge for at least 6 hours or ideally overnight.

When you're ready to serve, dip the mould in a bowl of hot water for a couple of seconds. Place a plate on top and flip it over to release the jelly.

MAKE AHEAD

The jelly can be made and stored in the fridge up to 3 days ahead.

lemon tart with basil cream

MAKE AHEAD

Make the lemon filling up to 2 days ahead and store in an airtight container in the fridge.
If you're really pressed for time, you can use a pre-made pastry shell.

A lemon tart is a beautifully delicate dessert. It's not too in-your-face but can certainly hold its own. A good lemon tart should have a well-pronounced lemon flavour but it shouldn't be so tart that it makes you wince (as did my first few attempts of this tart). The silky, buttery filling is zingy and fresh and would be perfect for a springtime evening dessert. A lightly infused basil cream brings some fragrance and playfulness that keeps people going back in for a second or third slice. For a bit of extra frill, I like to blitz some leftover basil leaves in a food processor with caster sugar, and sprinkle it on top.

Serves 12

For the filling

grated zest of 3 lemons and 175ml (6fl oz/¾ cup) lemon juice
220g (7¾oz/generous 1 cup) caster (superfine) sugar
3 eggs, plus 2 egg yolks
250g (9oz/1 cup plus 2 Tbsp) unsalted butter, very soft

For the basil cream

200g (8oz/scant 1 cup) double (heavy) cream
½ Tbsp icing (confectioners') sugar
6 basil leaves

For the pastry

200g (7oz/1½ cups) plain (all-purpose) flour, plus extra for dusting
110g (3¾oz/scant ½ cup) cold unsalted butter, diced
40g (1½oz/4½ Tbsp) icing (confectioners') sugar
pinch of fine sea salt
2 egg yolks

The filling will need plenty of time to chill, so make this first. Add the lemon zest and juice, the sugar, whole eggs and extra yolks to a heatproof bowl and give it a quick mix to combine. Place the bowl over a pan of simmering water and cook, stirring until it thickens enough to coat the back of a spoon. This can take up to 10–12 minutes, so be patient! If you're using a cooking thermometer, it will be done at about 77°C (170°F).

Let cool for 15 minutes before pouring it through a sieve (strainer) and into a blender. With the blender running, add chunks of the softened butter a little at a time, letting it incorporate before adding more.

Once all the butter has been added, pour the mixture into a bowl or container and cover with plastic wrap touching the surface. Chill in the fridge for 6 hours or overnight until it's well chilled and thickened.

To make the basil whip, add the cream, icing sugar and basil to a pan and heat gently until hot but not boiling. Remove from the heat, cover and let the basil infuse for at least 30 minutes. Remove the basil leaves and put the cream in the fridge until well chilled.

To make the pastry, add the flour, butter, icing sugar and salt to a food processor. Blitz until the mixture resembles fine breadcrumbs. Add in the yolks and pulse again until the mixture starts to clump together. Add a tablespoon of water if it still looks really dry.

Turn the mixture out onto a lightly floured surface and use your hands to bring it together. Pat it into a thick disc, wrap in plastic wrap and chill in the fridge for 2–3 hours or until firm.

Once chilled, roll out the pastry about 3–4mm (⅛in) thick. Roll it into a 23-cm (9-in) tart pan, making sure the pastry is pressed into all the crevices and there's a little overhang of pastry. Chill in the fridge for 30 minutes or in the freezer for 15 minutes.

Preheat the oven to 190°C (170°C fan/ 375°F/gas mark 5).

Use a fork to dock the base of the pastry and then line it with a sheet of baking paper. Fill with baking beans or uncooked rice and bake for 15–18 minutes until the edges have started to brown. Carefully remove the baking paper and beans and put the tart back in the oven for 10–12 minutes until the base looks dry and lightly browned.

Let it cool for a few minutes before using a sharp knife to trim off the excess pastry.

Fill the tart shell with the lemon filling mixture, smoothing the top with a palette knife. Place it back in the fridge for 30–60 minutes to set again.

To serve, lightly whip the chilled basil cream to get soft peaks, and dollop on the tart. Top with basil sugar (see introduction), if using.

my perfect crumble

So what makes a good crumble? It's all subjective, I know, but for me, I need a mix of apples. Bramleys can quickly turn to mush but you need some of that tartness to balance things out. So I like to add some dessert apples as well. I need a 60:40 ratio of crumble to fruit, and the crumble should be exactly that, crumbly. Nothing that's too sandy or fine, I want some clumps! And this is the time to use salted butter. Add just a little cinnamon and a pinch of nutmeg to flavour the apples and you've got yourself a 10/10 pudding. Put this in the oven while dinner is still going on so it's hot and bubbly in time for dessert.

Serves 6

For the apples

450g (14¼oz) eating apples (I use Braeburn)
80g (2¾oz/generous ⅓ cup) golden caster (superfine) sugar
½ tsp ground cinnamon
pinch of freshly grated nutmeg
1 tsp vanilla bean paste
350g (12oz) Bramley apples
2 Tbsp lemon juice
10g (¼oz/2 tsp) salted butter, plus extra for greasing

For the crumble

130g (4½oz[illegible]p) plain (all-purpose) flour
35g (1¼o[illegible]sp) golden caster (supe[illegible]ugar
30g ([illegible]cup) jumbo oats
110[illegible]oz/scant ½ cup) cold salted [illegible], diced

Preheat the oven to 200°C (180°C fan/400°F/gas mark 6).

Peel and core the eating apples and roughly chop them up. Add them to a bowl with half of the sugar, the cinnamon, nutmeg and vanilla. Give it all a good mix and set aside.

Peel and core the Bramley apples and roughly chop them up. Add them to a saucepan with the remaining sugar and the lemon juice. Cover the pan and cook gently over a medium heat until they start to soften but not turn to mush. Remove from the heat and stir in the butter.

Add the cooked apples to the raw apples and give it all a good mix. Pour it all into the base of a buttered baking dish to cool.

To make the crumble, add the flour, sugar and oats to a bowl. Add in the butter and use your fingertips to rub it into the flour until you have a clumpy mixture.

Tip the crumble on top of the apples. If you're making this ahead of time, chill in the fridge until you're ready to bake.

Bake for 45–50 minutes until the crumble is well browned and the fruit juices are bubbling up underneath. Let it cool for 10 minutes before serving warm, with ice cream or custard.

MAKE AHEAD

Make the crumble topping up to 3 days in advance and store in a food bag or container in the fridge. Once baked, it's best served on the same day.

poached quince & custard crumble cake

MAKE AHEAD

The quince can be poached 3 days ahead, the custard and crumble can be made 2 days ahead.

I had my first quince only a few years ago. It's not a fruit I was familiar with or grew up eating, but better late than never. They're not too dissimilar to a pear except much more fragrant and they're rarely eaten raw. When poached, they come alive, changing colour from off-white to a rosy pink and, with enough cooking, sometimes a deep ruby red. The recipe makes more quince than you need for the cake but you can eat the rest with yoghurt and granola, or serve on the side for those who like things extra fruity. There are a few different elements happening here but you can split them across a couple of days to make it more manageable.

Serves 9

For the poached quince
1.3 litres (44fl oz/5½ cups) water
pared zest (using a swivel peeler) and juice of 1 lemon
300g (10½oz/1½ cups) caster (superfine) sugar
1 star anise
6 cardamom pods, lightly bashed
2 ripe quince

For the custard
3 egg yolks
50g (1¾oz/¼ cup) caster (superfine) sugar
25g (1oz/2½ Tbsp) cornflour (cornstarch)
300ml (10½fl oz/generous 1¼ cups) milk
2 tsp vanilla bean paste

Start with poaching the quince. Add the water to a deep saucepan. Add the lemon zest and juice, sugar and spices and bring to the boil.

Wash and peel the quince, adding the peelings to the pan. Cut each quince into quarters and add them to the pan, turning the heat right down low. (I find it easier to remove the cores once they're cooked.) Cover the fruit with a round of baking paper and place the lid on top. Let the fruit simmer gently for 45–60 minutes or until the quince have softened and a sharp knife can easily pierce into the flesh.

Remove from the heat and let the quince cool completely in the liquid. Once cool, discard the peel, pour the fruit and its liquid into a container and store in the fridge until ready to use.

To make the custard, beat the yolks and sugar together in a bowl until smooth. Mix in the cornflour until you don't have any lumps. Heat the milk and vanilla in a small saucepan until steaming, but don't let it come to the boil. Pour a third of the milk onto the eggs, whisking to combine. Continue adding the milk a little at a time, while whisking, until you've added it all. Pour everything back into the saucepan and heat gently, stirring continuously. The custard will start to thicken after 2–3 minutes. Once it starts bubbling, remove from the heat and pour into a clean bowl. Cover with some plastic wrap touching the surface and set aside to cool. Chill in the fridge until needed.

continued overleaf

poached quince & custard crumble cake continued

For the crumble
1 tsp fennel seeds
80g (2¾oz/scant ⅔ cup) plain (all-purpose) flour
20g (¾oz/¼ cup) jumbo oats
50g (1¾oz/3½ Tbsp) unsalted butter
30g (1oz/2½ Tbsp) caster (superfine) sugar

For the cake
125g (4½oz/½ cup plus 1 Tbsp) unsalted butter, softened, plus extra for greasing
150g (5½oz/¾ cup) caster (superfine) sugar
2 eggs
160g (5¾oz/scant 1¼ cups) plain (all-purpose) flour
50g (1¾oz/scant ½ cup) ground almonds
1 tsp baking powder
½ tsp bicarbonate of soda (baking soda)
¼ tsp fine sea salt
80g (2¾oz/⅓ cup) sour cream

For the crumble, grind the fennel seeds in a pestle and mortar to get a coarsely ground mixture. Add this to a bowl along with all the other crumble ingredients. Use your fingers to rub the butter into the dry ingredients until you have a clumpy, chunky mixture. Cover and chill until needed.

When you're ready to make the cake, preheat the oven to 180°C (160°C fan/350°F/gas mark 4). Grease a 20-cm (8-in) square baking pan and line with baking paper, leaving enough overhang to help you lift it out later.

Cream the butter and sugar together for 3–4 minutes until pale and creamy. Add the eggs one at a time, beating well after each. Tip in the flour, almonds, baking powder, bicarbonate of soda and salt. Mix to get a thick batter before stirring in the sour cream. Spoon the batter into the pan, smoothing it out evenly.

Give the custard a good whisk to remove any lumps and dollop it across the surface of the cake.

You only need half the quince for this cake. Remove the cores from the quince and slice into pieces about 1cm (½in) thick. Lay the quince gently on top of the custard and sprinkle the crumble on top, letting some of the fruit and custard poke through.

Bake for 45–55 minutes until there isn't any wobble and the crumble is nice and golden.

Let it cool completely before slicing so the custard has time to set.

Serve at room temperature, or double down and serve with more hot custard.

saffron & cardamom pear galettes

I'll always have time for a galette. Even more so when they're mini and I get a whole one to myself. They're a lot less pressure if you don't want or need to make a whole pie, and sturdy enough to transport easily without worrying about leaks and spills. I love using a bit of wholemeal flour in these for that nutty texture it brings to the pastry, but feel free to use just plain (all-purpose) flour if preferred. Bring these along for a smaller, cosy gathering and serve warm with crème fraîche, ice cream or sour cream crème pât (page 179).

Serves 4

For the poached pears
4 ripe but firm pears
700ml (23½fl oz/3 cups) water
225g (8oz/generous 1 cup) caster (superfine) sugar
20g (¾oz) fresh ginger, finely sliced
10 green cardamom pods
pinch of saffron strands

Peel your pears and cut them in half. Remove the core and set aside.

Add the water, sugar, ginger and cardamom to a deep saucepan and bring to the boil. Add in the saffron and reduce the heat to a simmer.

Place your pears in the liquid, cover with the lid slightly ajar and poach for 20–30 minutes, until softened but still holding their shape. Remove from the heat and let the pears cool in the syrup. If you're making ahead, place the pears and syrup in the fridge until needed.

To make the pastry, add both flours to a bowl. Mix in the salt and sugar. Add in the diced butter and use your fingertips to rub it into the flour until you have a coarse breadcrumb mixture. Make a well in the centre and add 50ml (2fl oz/3½ Tbsp) water. Use a table knife to stir and bring it together to get a rough dough. If it still looks really dry, add in a bit more water, a tablespoon at a time.

Turn it out onto a lightly floured surface and use your hands to bring it together into a thick disc. Wrap in plastic wrap and chill in the fridge for 3–4 hours or overnight.

On the day you're baking, line 2 baking trays with baking paper.

Cut your dough into 4 pieces and roll each one out, about 15cm (6in) wide. Place 2 on each baking tray and dust the base with some ground almonds, leaving about 2.5cm (1in) clear around the edges.

MAKE AHEAD

Best served on the day they are made, but you can make the pastry dough up to 2 days ahead and store it wrapped in the fridge. The pears can be poached up to 3 days ahead and stored in the fridge.

continued overleaf

saffron & cardamom pear galettes continued

For the pastry

100g (3½oz/¾ cup) plain (all-purpose) flour, plus extra for dusting
100g (3½oz/¾ cup) wholemeal (wholewheat) flour
pinch of fine sea salt
35g (1¼oz/2½ Tbsp) caster (superfine) sugar
120g (4¼oz/½ cup) cold unsalted butter, diced
50–60ml (2fl oz/3½–4 Tbsp) water
2 Tbsp ground almonds
1 egg, beaten
handful of flaked (slivered) almonds
2 Tbsp demerara (turbinado) sugar

Remove the pears from the syrup and slice each half diagonally into about 5 slices. Arrange 2 halves (so about 10 slices) on each pastry disc and fold the edges up and over some of the fruit. Chill the galettes for 20 minutes.

Preheat the oven to 200°C (180°C fan/ 400°F/gas mark 6). Brush the pastry with the beaten egg and sprinkle the flaked almonds and demerara sugar on top.

Bake for 30–35 minutes until the pastry is golden. Let them cool completely on a wire rack before serving or boxing up in an airtight container.

You'll have a lot of poaching liquid left over. You can strain this and add it back to a saucepan, bring to the boil and let it reduce by about two-thirds. Serve the galettes with a drizzle of the syrup if you want something sweeter, or it can be used for drinks.

apricot & chamomile tart

A really good, raw apricot can be hard to come by. They're often a little disappointing, neither here nor there. But when poached or roasted, they turn into something magnificent. Here, they're gently poached in chamomile tea for something bright and floral that sits on top of a creamy, tangy filling. The base is perfect for people who don't like making pastry – no rolling or chilling required and you're left with a buttery, crunchy case to hold it all together.

Serves 8–10

For the base

- 120g (4¼oz/½ cup) cold salted butter, diced, plus extra for greasing
- 175g (6oz/1⅓ cups) plain (all-purpose) flour
- 60g (2¼oz/7 Tbsp) icing (confectioners') sugar

For the apricots

- 3 chamomile tea bags
- 100g (3½oz/½ cup) caster (superfine) sugar
- 200ml (7fl oz/scant 1 cup) water
- juice of ½ lemon
- 6 apricots, halved and pitted

For the filling

- 330g (11½oz/1½ cups) cream cheese
- 120g (4¼oz/½ cup) sour cream
- 4 Tbsp icing (confectioners') sugar
- 2 tsp vanilla bean paste
- grated zest of 1 lemon

Preheat the oven to 190°C (170°C fan/ 375°F/gas mark 5). Lightly grease a 23-cm (9-in) baking dish or pan.

To make the base, add the flour and icing sugar to a large bowl and mix to combine. Rub the butter into the flour using your fingertips until the mixture looks really fine. Use your hands to start bringing the dough together; it should start clumping quite easily.

Tip the dough into your dish and press it evenly in the base and sides. Use the back of a spoon to smooth the base, making sure it's all firmly packed.

Prick the base with a fork and bake for 20–25 minutes (it'll take longer in a ceramic dish so keep an eye on it) until the edges have started to brown and the base looks dry to the touch. Remove from the oven and set aside to cool completely.

For the apricots, add the tea bags, sugar, water and lemon juice to a saucepan and bring to the boil. Let it simmer for 3–4 minutes before turning the heat down to low and adding in the apricots. Let them poach very gently in the liquid for 8–10 minutes. You want them to soften but still hold their shape – if they're really unripe, it will take a little longer.

Remove from the heat and let the apricots cool in the poaching liquid. Chill in the fridge until needed.

To make the filling, add all the ingredients to a bowl and mix until smooth. Spoon the filling into the pastry-lined dish and then top with the apricots. Chill until you're ready to serve.

MAKE AHEAD

Make the base up to 2 days in advance and store in an airtight container. Don't fill the tart until the day you're planning to serve it.

last-minute strawberries & cream

MAKE AHEAD

This needs to be made on the day.

This is a pudding for those times when you literally have no time. When even thinking about turning on the oven or bringing out all your equipment is just too much. Or when you've completely forgotten you said you'd bring something along. We've all been there and this is the answer. It's a dessert that's so incredibly low effort but no one would know, or even care, because it tastes so good. Let the strawberries macerate and get all syrupy, and just whip up a bit of cream with lemon curd folded in. Serve with some shop-bought biscuits (cookies) on the side if you want a little crunch.

Serves 4

300g (10½oz) strawberries, hulled and halved
40g (1½oz/3¼ Tbsp) caster (superfine) sugar
squeeze of lemon juice
1 tsp vanilla bean paste
300ml (10½fl oz/generous 1¼ cups) double (heavy) cream
2 Tbsp lemon curd
fresh mint leaves, to serve

Add the strawberries, sugar, lemon juice and vanilla to a bowl or Tupperware and mix to coat. Cover and let the strawberries macerate for at least 30 minutes. They'll become softened and syrupy. Chill until needed.

Lightly whip the cream until you have very soft peaks. Stir through the lemon curd and chill until needed.

Serve the strawberries with a dollop of cream and some of the syrup from the strawberries. Top with fresh mint leaves.

something chocolatey

I can never resist a chocolate dessert, even more so when it's homemade. There's usually always one person that will declare their dislike for chocolate but there are a range of recipes in this chapter that have varying degrees of richness so there's something for everyone. For something lighter, try the clotted cream and chocolate chip cake (page 92). And for the proper chocolate lovers, bring along the crispy chocolate & dulce de leche tart (page 91) and you'll be the favourite person in the room.

chocolate buttermilk traybake with muscovado frosting & thyme caramel

MAKE AHEAD

Make the cake up to 2 days ahead and wrap well to store. The caramel can be made up to 5 days ahead, but make the buttercream on the day you are serving.

Traybakes or sheet cakes tick many boxes when you're on dessert duty. Cut slices up as small or as large as you need to feed a crowd. The buttermilk sponge has a soft, tender crumb that delivers on the chocolate flavour but still lets the earthy muscovado buttercream shine. The thyme caramel takes chocolate cake up a couple of notches, so don't skip it if you've got the time! I tend to leave the cake in the pan it was baked in and decorate it in there too, for ease of transporting.

Serves 16–20

For the cake

100g (3½oz/scant ½ cup) unsalted butter, plus extra for greasing
100g (3½oz) dark chocolate, roughly chopped
300ml (10½fl oz/generous 1¼ cups) buttermilk
2 eggs
280g (10oz/generous 2 cups) plain (all-purpose) flour
280g (10oz/scant 1½ cups) light muscovado sugar
50g (1¾oz/½ cup) unsweetened cocoa powder
1 tsp baking powder
1½ tsp bicarbonate of soda (baking soda)
¼ tsp fine sea salt
200ml (7fl oz/scant 1 cup) hot water

Preheat the oven to 180°C (160°C fan/ 350°F/gas mark 4). Grease a 23 x 33-cm (9 x 13-in) round cake pan and line with baking paper, leaving enough overhang to help you pull it out later.

Add the butter and chocolate to a heatproof bowl and melt in short bursts in the microwave or set over a pan of simmering water. Set aside to cool a little.

Mix the buttermilk and eggs together in a small jug (pitcher) and set aside.

Add the flour, sugar, cocoa powder, baking powder, bicarbonate of soda and salt to a bowl and mix to combine. Make a well in the centre and pour in the buttermilk mixture followed by the melted chocolate. Give it a good mix until you have a smooth, thick batter. Pour in the hot water and gently stir to combine.

Pour the batter into the prepared cake pan and bake for 40–45 minutes or until a skewer inserted into the middle comes out clean. Set aside to cool completely in the pan.

To make the caramel, add the cream and thyme to a small saucepan and heat gently until warmed through. Remove from the heat and cover to let it infuse for at least 20 minutes, although an hour is preferred.

Strain the cream and set it aside. Clean your saucepan and add in the sugar. Heat gently until the sugar melts and turns a deep amber colour. Give the pan a swirl every now and then to help it melt evenly.

continued overleaf

chocolate buttermilk traybake with muscovado frosting & thyme caramel continued

For the thyme caramel

150ml (5fl oz/scant ⅔ cup) double (heavy) cream
5 sprigs of fresh thyme, plus extra to decorate
100g (3½oz/½ cup) golden caster (superfine) sugar
50g (2oz/scant ¼ cup) unsalted butter, softened
pinch of flaky sea salt

For the Swiss meringue buttercream

180g (6¼oz) egg whites (from 4–5 large eggs)
240g (8½oz/1¼ cups) light muscovado sugar
335g (11¾oz/1½ cups) unsalted butter, softened
¼ tsp fine sea salt

Add in the butter – the sugar will spit and bubble so be careful – and mix quickly to combine. Slowly pour in the cream while stirring, and then let the caramel bubble away for 30 seconds. Remove from the heat and add the salt. Let it cool completely.

To make the Swiss meringue buttercream, add the egg whites and sugar to the bowl of a stand mixer. Place the bowl over a pan of simmering water, making sure the bottom of the bowl isn't touching the water.

Keep the water at a simmer while whisking the egg whites. Once the sugar has dissolved and the egg whites are hot to the touch, remove from the heat. Whisk the whites on high speed until they are thick and glossy and the bowl is cool to touch.

With the mixer still running, add in all the softened butter and salt. The mixture will deflate and look a bit curdled but as you keep whisking it will come together. If after 5 minutes the buttercream looks really soupy, stick it in the fridge for 20 minutes and then continue to whip. Once the buttercream is smooth and silky, mix on low speed for about a minute to remove any large air bubbles.

To assemble, spoon the buttercream onto the cake, adding some swirls and swoops with a palette knife or the back of a spoon. Drizzle some caramel on top and decorate with a few sprigs of thyme.

chocolate, cherry & Amaretto cream cake

This is a bit of a riff on the classic Black Forest gâteau. And classics are classics for a reason. Chocolate and cherries will always be great friends, and pour in some sweet Amaretto, add a feather-light sponge and lots of fresh cream and you've got yourself a winner. This can easily be dressed up with candles or even sparklers to be a proper celebration cake. A good one to bring along when you want to impress.

Serves 10–12

85g (3oz/⅔ cup) plain (all-purpose) flour
30g (1oz/4 Tbsp) unsweetened cocoa powder
¼ tsp fine sea salt
4 eggs
100g (3½oz/½ cup) caster (superfine) sugar
chocolate shavings, to finish
handful of crushed amaretti biscuits, to finish

For the cherries

350g (12oz) pitted cherries, fresh or frozen, plus extra to decorate
40g (1½oz/3¼ Tbsp) caster (superfine) sugar
1 star anise
juice of ½ lemon
100ml (3½fl oz/scant ½ cup) Amaretto

Preheat the oven to 190°C (170°C fan/ 375°F/gas mark 5).

Line a 30 x 20-cm (12 x 8-in) Swiss roll (jelly roll) pan with baking paper.

To make the cake, sift the flour, cocoa powder and salt together and set aside.

Add the eggs and sugar to the bowl of a stand mixer and whisk on high speed for 4–5 minutes until the eggs are really thick and pale and doubled in size. You want the eggs to get to ribbon stage – when you lift the whisk attachment, the eggs should leave a trail on the surface before disappearing.

Sift the flour onto the eggs in 2 batches, being very gentle to fold it in after each addition. Pockets of flour like to hide at the bottom, so make sure it's fully combined without knocking out too much air.

Pour the batter into the prepared pan and bake for 20–25 minutes until the surface looks dry and puffy. Remove from the oven and set aside to cool completely.

Add all the ingredients for the cherries except the Amaretto to a small pan and bring to the boil. Let it simmer for 5–6 minutes until the cherries look syrupy. Remove from the heat, stir in the Amaretto and set aside to cool.

MAKE AHEAD

The sponge can be made 2 days ahead, and the cherries 5 days ahead, and stored in the fridge.

The finished cake needs to be stored in the fridge due to the fresh cream.

continued overleaf

chocolate, cherry & Amaretto cream cake continued

For the chocolate frosting

170g (6oz) dark chocolate
85g (3oz/⅓ cup plus 2 tsp) unsalted butter
100g (3½oz/½ cup) light brown sugar
100ml (3½fl oz/scant ½ cup) hot water
25g (1oz/3½ Tbsp) unsweetened cocoa powder
pinch of fine sea salt

For the cream

250ml (9fl oz/generous 1 cup) double (heavy) cream
60g (2oz/¼ cup) sour cream
1 tsp vanilla bean paste
1 Tbsp icing (confectioners') sugar

To make the frosting, add all the ingredients to a clean pan and heat gently until melted, stirring occasionally. Pour it into a bowl and let it cool for a few hours until it thickens to a spreadable consistency. You can speed this up by placing it in the fridge and stirring every so often.

Make the cream by adding the cream, sour cream, vanilla and icing sugar to a bowl and whipping until you have stiff peaks.

When you're ready to assemble, slice the cake in half lengthways and place it straight on the plate or board you'll serve it on. Spoon the syrup from the cherries onto each cake, letting it completely soak into the sponge. Fold half of the cherries into the cream before spooning it onto the base cake and top with the remaining cherries.

Place the second cake on top, then spoon and spread the frosting over the top and sides. Top with chocolate shavings, extra cherries and crushed amaretti biscuits.

halva & smoked salt chocolate cookies

Cookies for dessert are a little underrated. They're low key and unfussy but always very popular. Bring out a tray of warm cookies after dinner and watch everyone go weak at the knees. For the halva lovers, you can serve these with a scoop of ice cream and more halva crumbled on top. Or double up on the chocolate and add a drizzle of the hot chocolate sauce on page 124.

Makes 12

125g (4½oz/½ cup plus 1 Tbsp) unsalted butter, softened
75g (2½oz/6 Tbsp) caster (superfine) sugar
120g (4¼oz/scant ⅔ cup) light brown sugar
1 egg
200g (7oz/1½ cups) plain (all-purpose) flour
30g (1oz/scant ⅓ cup) unsweetened cocoa powder
½ tsp baking powder
½ tsp bicarbonate of soda (baking soda)
½ tsp smoked salt, plus extra to finish
100g (3½oz) dark chocolate, roughly chopped
100g (3½oz) halva

Add the butter and both sugars to a bowl and cream with a stand mixer or electric whisk until pale and fluffy. Add in the egg and beat until combined.

In a separate bowl, mix together the flour, cocoa powder, baking powder, bicarbonate of soda and salt. Tip this into the butter mixture and mix on low speed until just combined. Stir in the chopped dark chocolate.

Scoop the dough into 12 balls and place them on a baking sheet lined with baking paper. Cover with plastic wrap and chill in the fridge for 2–3 hours or until firm. (You can also chill overnight.)

Preheat the oven to 180°C (160°C fan/ 350°F/gas mark 4).

Split your halva evenly into 12 chunks. Taking one ball of dough at a time, flatten it a little in the palm of your hand. Place the halva in the middle and pinch the dough together to seal it in. Place it seam side down on the baking sheet. Repeat with the rest of the dough and halva and bake the cookies in batches for 12–15 minutes until the edges are set but the middle is still a bit soft.

Sprinkle over some more smoked salt and serve the cookies warm with ice cream or on their own.

MAKE AHEAD

The dough can be made up to 2 days ahead and stored in the fridge.

tahini, date & chocolate pudding

MAKE AHEAD

Make the cake the day before and reheat gently in the oven.

This is a warm, sweet, sticky pudding that's the sort of dessert you scooch over to the sofas for. Think sticky toffee pud but a little different. The tahini brings a gorgeous nutty flavour and there's a gentle hint of chocolate here that isn't too overwhelming. Scoop this generously into bowls and let it soak up lots of toffee-like chocolate sauce.

Serves 6–8

80ml (2½fl oz/⅓ cup) neutral oil (such as sunflower or vegetable), plus extra for greasing
130g (4¾oz) pitted dates, roughly chopped
200ml (7fl oz/scant 1 cup) oat milk
1 tsp bicarbonate of soda (baking soda)
100g (3½oz/½ cup) dark muscovado sugar
50g (3½oz/½ cup) caster (superfine) sugar
70g (2½oz) tahini, plus extra to drizzle
50ml (2fl oz/3½ Tbsp) hot water
1½ tsp apple cider vinegar
150g (5½oz/1 cup plus 2 Tbsp) plain (all-purpose) flour
20g (¾oz/3 Tbsp) unsweetened cocoa powder
1 tsp baking powder
2 tsp ground ginger
¼ tsp ground cloves
½ tsp fine sea salt
2 Tbsp sesame seeds

For the sauce

200g (7oz/1 cup) dark muscovado sugar
175ml (6fl oz/¾ cup) double (heavy) cream (or plant-based)
50g (1¾oz/3½ Tbsp) salted butter (or plant-based)
50g (1¾oz) dark chocolate, roughly chopped

Preheat the oven to 180°C (160°C fan/ 350°F/gas mark 4). Lightly grease an oval oven dish, about 26 x 18cm (10 x 7in).

Add the dates and oat milk to a saucepan and heat gently for 4–5 minutes or until the dates are well softened. Add to a food processor with the bicarbonate of soda and blitz until smooth.

Add the oil, sugars and tahini to a bowl and mix to combine. Stir in the hot water, followed by the date mixture and apple cider vinegar.

In a separate bowl, mix together the flour, cocoa powder, baking powder, ginger, cloves and salt. Make a well in the centre and pour in the wet mixture, stirring until just combined.

Pour the batter into the prepared dish. Top with the sesame seeds and bake for 30–35 minutes.

To make the sauce, add the sugar, cream and butter to a small saucepan and heat gently until melted. Let it simmer for 2 minutes before stirring in the chocolate until melted.

Serve the cake warm with lots of sauce, an extra drizzle of tahini and a scoop of ice cream.

Irish cream chocolate mousse

If you're a proper chocolate lover, then having a good mousse recipe up your sleeve is a must. This is rich and airy with a good hit of Irish cream for a post dinner treat. There are so few ingredients in this that now is a good time to crack out the good chocolate.

Things move quickly when making a mousse, so make sure you've got everything weighed out ready to go. As it is quite rich, I sometimes also make this in one big dish instead of ramekins, and let everyone serve themselves with as much or as little as they want.

Serves 6

120g (4¼oz) dark chocolate
4 eggs, separated
50ml (2fl oz/3½ Tbsp) Irish cream
pinch of fine sea salt
40g (1½oz/3¼ Tbsp) caster (superfine) sugar
unsweetened cocoa powder or shaved dark chocolate, to finish

Add the chocolate to a heatproof bowl and set it over a pan of simmering water to melt. Alternatively, melt it in short bursts in the microwave. Set aside to cool a little.

Add the egg yolks to a separate bowl and pour in the Irish cream. Give it a quick mix to combine.

Add the egg whites and salt to another clean, grease-free bowl. Start whisking until they are frothy with soft peaks. Keep whisking while you add in the sugar a tablespoon at a time and the egg whites are thickened and glossy. You don't need to take them all the way to stiff peaks.

Pour the chocolate into the egg yolks and mix quickly to combine. Add a spoonful of egg whites to the chocolate mixture and mix it in to loosen up the chocolate.

Add the rest of the egg whites in 3 batches, carefully folding each in to combine. Try not to knock out too much air.

Pour the mousse into 6 ramekins and chill in the fridge for 4 hours, or overnight.

To serve, top with a dusting of cocoa powder or some shaved chocolate.

MAKE AHEAD

Make up to 2 days ahead and store covered in the fridge.

white chocolate & rosewater mud cake

MAKE AHEAD

Make the cake up to 2 days ahead and add the glaze before serving.

Mud cake gets its name from the texture of the crumb – it's beautifully dense in the very best way. There's a lot of white chocolate in this but it's surprisingly not as sweet as you might expect, I promise. The chocolate brings a velvety texture and the rosewater does a graceful job of cutting through a bit of the richness. This is one that benefits from being made in advance; it gets even better the next day, so take advantage of that.

Serves 8–10

120g (4¼oz/½ cup) unsalted butter, plus extra for greasing
200g (7oz) white chocolate, roughly chopped
160ml (5¼fl oz/⅔ cup) milk
140g (5oz/¾ cup minus 2 tsp) caster (superfine) sugar
2 eggs
1½ tsp rosewater
175g (6oz/1⅓ cups) plain (all-purpose) flour
1½ tsp baking powder
¼ tsp fine sea salt
dried rose petals, to decorate

For the glaze

75g (2½oz) white chocolate
1½ Tbsp milk

Preheat the oven to 170°C (150°C fan/325°F/gas mark 3). Grease a deep 15-cm (6-in) round cake pan and line with baking paper.

Add the butter, chocolate and milk to a heatproof bowl and set it over a pan of simmering water to melt, stirring occasionally. Or melt in short bursts in the microwave. Once melted, set aside to cool a little.

Stir in the sugar, followed by the eggs and rosewater, and mix to combine.

Add in the flour, baking powder and salt and mix to get a smooth batter.

Pour the batter into the prepared cake pan and bake for 55–60 minutes until well risen and a deep brown colour.

Let it cool in the pan for 10 minutes before turning it out onto a wire rack to cool completely.

To make the glaze, add the chocolate and milk to a heatproof bowl and set it over a pan of simmering water. Let it melt gently, stirring occasionally.

Pour the glaze over the cooled cake, top with dried rose petals and let it set before slicing.

chocolate & coconut breadcrumb cake

MAKE AHEAD

Make up to 2 days ahead and keep well wrapped.

Most recipes that use breadcrumbs extol them as back-up options if you've got leftover bread, but as a carb lover this is never an issue for me. I'll happily buy a loaf of bread just so I can make this cake. The breadcrumbs give it a soft, squidgy texture that tastes delightful and almost pudding-like. It's a cake that can be dressed up or down depending on what you fancy. Keep it plain or serve with chocolate custard (page 178) and toasted coconut flakes. Whichever way you go, I think it's best served warm, so if you've made it in advance, give it a few seconds in the microwave to bring it back to life.

Serves 8–10

- 130g (4¾oz/½ cup plus 1 Tbsp) coconut oil, plus extra for greasing
- 40g (1½oz/½ cup) desiccated (grated unsweetened) coconut
- 60ml (2fl oz/4 Tbsp) hot water
- 120g (4¼oz/scant ⅔ cup) light brown sugar
- 2 eggs
- 30g (1oz/4 Tbsp) unsweetened cocoa powder
- 20g (¾oz/2⅓ Tbsp) plain (all-purpose) flour
- 1½ tsp baking powder
- ¼ tsp fine sea salt
- 100g (3½oz/2 cups) fresh breadcrumbs
- toasted coconut flakes, to serve (optional)

Preheat the oven to 180°C (160°C fan/ 350°F/gas mark 4). Grease a 20-cm (8-in) round cake pan and line with baking paper.

Add the desiccated coconut to a small bowl and pour over 40ml (1¼fl oz/ 2½ Tbsp) of the hot water. Let it sit for 5 minutes so the coconut can hydrate.

Gently melt the coconut oil in bursts in the microwave, or in a small saucepan. Add it to a bowl with the sugar and mix until combined. Mix in the eggs.

Add in the cocoa powder, flour, baking powder and salt and stir to combine before mixing in the desiccated coconut and breadcrumbs. Stir in the remaining hot water and pour the batter into the prepared cake pan.

Bake for 25–30 minutes or until a skewer inserted into the centre comes out clean.

Serve warm with cold cream, or with the chocolate custard on page 178, and some toasted coconut flakes, if you like.

chocolate brownie pudding with cornflake crunch

MAKE AHEAD

Make all elements up to 3 days ahead. Store the brownies and custard in the fridge and the cornflakes in an airtight container at room temperature.

This is not for the faint hearted. Rich and indulgent, and a little over the top, in the best way. When I was younger and going for dinner at TGI Fridays, which felt like the height of coolness, my sister and I would always share the brownie sundae. In a glass the size of our heads was a tooth-achingly sweet mess of brownie chunks, chocolate sauce, caramel sauce, toffee popcorn and ice cream. The thought of it now does make my teeth ache but we loved it. I've downsized and tidied up this version but still kept the playfulness. This is very much an assembly sort of pudding: buy a tub of vanilla ice cream, and let everyone make their own.

Serves 6–8

For the brownies

120g (4¼oz/½ cup) unsalted butter, plus extra for greasing
120g (4¼oz) dark chocolate
1 Tbsp unsweetened cocoa powder
200g (7oz/1 cup) light brown sugar
2 eggs
75g (2½oz/½ cup plus 1 Tbsp) plain (all-purpose) flour
¼ tsp fine sea salt

For the chocolate custard

4 egg yolks
70g (2½oz/generous ⅓ cup) caster (superfine) sugar
15g (½oz/1½ Tbsp) cornflour (cornstarch)
2 tsp unsweetened cocoa powder
400ml (14fl oz/1¾ cups) milk
pinch of fine sea salt
½ tsp instant coffee
40g (1½oz) dark chocolate, chopped

For the cornflake crunch

50g (1¾oz/¼ cup) caster (superfine) sugar
1 Tbsp water
25g (1oz) hazelnuts, roughly chopped
25g (1½oz) cornflakes

To serve

ice cream

For the brownies, preheat the oven to 180°C (160°C fan/350°F/gas mark 4). Grease a 20-cm (8-in) square cake pan and line with baking paper.

Add the butter, chocolate and cocoa powder to a heatproof bowl and place it over a pan of simmering water, stirring gently until it's completely melted. Set aside.

Add the sugar and eggs to a bowl and mix until smooth. Stir in the chocolate mixture and then mix in the flour and salt until you have a smooth batter. Pour the batter into the tin and bake for 18–23 minutes or until the edges are firm but the middle is still a little soft. Remove from the oven and set aside to cool completely. I like to chill these in the fridge until I'm ready to use, so I can cut the brownies into neat little squares.

To make the custard, add the egg yolks, sugar, cornflour and cocoa powder to a heatproof bowl and whisk until smooth.

Add the milk and salt to a small saucepan and heat until steaming but not boiling. Stir in the instant coffee to dissolve. Pour half of the hot milk onto the eggs while whisking to quickly combine. Slowly pour in the rest of the milk while whisking continuously.

Pour everything back into the pan and heat it gently while stirring, until the custard starts to thicken. Once it comes to the boil and starts to bubble, remove from the heat and stir in the chopped chocolate until it melts. Pour it into a clean, shallow bowl and cover with plastic wrap, so it touches the surface of the custard. Let it cool to room temperature before chilling in the fridge.

To make the cornflake crunch, line a small baking tray with baking paper and set aside. Add the sugar and water to a pan and heat gently until the sugar is melted and the mixture comes to the boil. Tip in the chopped nuts and cornflakes and stir to coat. The mixture will look like it has crystallized but keep stirring until the sugar melts into a deep amber colour and coats the cornflakes.

Remove from the heat and pour it onto the lined tray to cool completely. Be careful here as the mixture will be extremely hot. Once cool, break up the cornflakes into smaller chunks.

When you're ready to assemble, slice the brownie into small chunks and give the custard a good whisk to remove any lumps. Layer up the elements in small ramekins and top with a scoop of ice cream and more cornflake crunch.

FORCE GOOD
£250,000
CHARITY
CARBON
WIN

white chocolate, rye & pretzel cookie

Homemade cookies are truly wonderful, but a giant homemade cookie still warm and gooey from the oven is on another level. This is the sort of thing I'd bring to a girly catch up where we can eat it straight from the pan while binge-watching *Real Housewives*. The edges are perfectly chewy with chunks of white chocolate running throughout, balancing the salty, crunchy pretzels. I include rye flour here and love the texture and nuttiness it brings. Once completely cool, you can slice up into cookie bars, but it's definitely best when warm.

Serves 6

140g (5oz/⅔ cup minus 2 tsp) unsalted butter, plus extra for greasing
100g (3½oz/½ cup) light brown sugar
70g (2½oz/generous ⅓ cup) caster (superfine) sugar
½ tsp vanilla bean paste
1 egg
100g (3½oz/¾ cup) wholemeal rye flour (not dark)
75g (2½oz/½ cup plus 1 Tbsp) plain (all-purpose) flour
2 tsp malted milk powder (such as Horlicks)
½ tsp fine sea salt
½ tsp bicarbonate of soda (baking soda)
140g (5oz) white chocolate, chopped
45g (1½oz) salted pretzels
flaky sea salt, to finish

Add the butter to a small saucepan over a medium heat. Continue to heat until the butter gets foamy and starts to smell nutty and fragrant. Once it turns a deep brown colour, remove from the heat and pour into a heatproof bowl. Let it cool to room temperature before placing in the fridge to firm up to a soft, spreadable consistency.

Preheat the oven to 200°C (180°C fan/ 400°F/gas mark 6). Grease a shallow 23-cm (9-in) round cake pan or skillet.

Add the softened brown butter to a bowl along with both sugars and the vanilla. Beat for 2–3 minutes until creamy and fluffy. Beat in the egg, mixing to combine.

In a separate bowl, sift together the rye flour, plain flour, malted milk powder, salt and bicarbonate of soda. Tip this into the butter mixture and stir to get a thick but soft dough.

Stir in the white chocolate pieces and three-quarters of the pretzels. Press the dough into your cake pan and top with the remaining pretzels.

Sprinkle with a little flaky sea salt and bake for 20–25 minutes until the edges are set and the middle is just a little soft. If you want your cookie extra gooey, bake for 2–3 minutes less.

Let it cool a little for 5 minutes before serving warm with ice cream.

MAKE AHEAD

The cookie dough can be made 2 days ahead and stored in the fridge. Take along the uncooked dough in the tin and stick it in the oven when needed so it stays warm and gooey in time for dessert.

spiced orange chocolate mousse cake

MAKE AHEAD

Make the cake and the oranges up to 2 days in advance.

I love a good flourless chocolate cake and have developed quite a few of them over the years, all slightly different in texture and taste. As the name suggests, this version is more mousse-like. Airy and light with warming spices and macerated oranges, it's a great one for the festive season.

Serves 10–12

175g (6oz/¾ cup) unsalted butter, plus extra for greasing
275g (9¾oz) dark chocolate, plus extra for grating
1½ tsp ground cinnamon
¼ tsp freshly grated nutmeg
4 eggs, separated
100g (3½oz/½ cup) caster (superfine) sugar
grated zest of 1 orange
15g (½oz/2 Tbsp) unsweetened cocoa powder

For the oranges

2 oranges
40g (1½oz/3¼ Tbsp) caster (superfine) sugar
50ml (2fl oz/3½ Tbsp) Grand Marnier or Triple Sec (optional)
1 small cinnamon stick
1 star anise

Preheat the oven to 180°C (160°C fan/350°F/gas mark 4). Grease a 20-cm (8-in) loose-bottomed, deep round cake pan and line with baking paper.

Add the butter, chocolate, cinnamon and nutmeg to a heatproof bowl. Place the bowl over a pan of simmering water and melt gently. Remove from the heat and set aside to cool.

In a separate bowl, whisk the egg yolks with half the sugar, the orange zest and cocoa powder. Whisk until the eggs are thick and pale, about 2–3 minutes. Pour the cooled chocolate into the yolks and mix until smooth.

Add the egg whites to another clean, grease-free bowl, or the bowl of a stand mixer. Whisk until frothy then, with the mixer or electric whisk still running, add in the remaining sugar 1 tablespoon at a time. Once you've added in all the sugar, fold about a quarter of the whites into the chocolate mixture. The first batch of egg whites is to loosen the mixture so you don't need to be too careful about knocking out air.

Gently fold in the rest of the egg whites. Then pour the batter into the prepared cake pan. Bake for 40–45 minutes until the cake looks risen and the edges are set. There should still be a little wobble in the middle.

Remove from the oven and set aside to cool completely.

To prepare the oranges, slice the top and bottom off of each one. Sit them upright and use a small, sharp knife to slice away the skin and pith, following the curve of the fruit. Cut between the membranes to remove the segments.

Toss the orange segments with the sugar, Grand Marnier, if using, cinnamon stick and star anise. Let it macerate in the fridge for at least an hour or overnight.

Serve slices of cake with the orange segments and some of the syrup, along with some crème fraîche and gratings of dark chocolate.

date night cake

This is the cutest little chocolate cake. Baked in a small cake pan, it's the perfect size for two people to share with just enough for leftovers, because chocolate cake for breakfast is truly one of life's simple pleasures. I've kept it very classic with a simple American buttercream and no extra frills, because it just doesn't need it. Although, maybe a few sprinkles could be fun. Get into it with a couple of forks; this isn't one I ever bother slicing.

Serves 2, with leftovers

For the cake

80g (2¾oz/scant ⅔ cup) plain (all-purpose) flour
100g (3½oz/½ cup) light brown sugar
20g (¾oz/3 Tbsp) unsweetened cocoa powder
½ tsp baking powder
¼ tsp bicarbonate of soda (baking soda)
¼ tsp fine sea salt
1 egg
60ml (2fl oz/¼ cup) milk
60ml (2fl oz/¼ cup) neutral oil (such as sunflower or vegetable)
60ml (2fl oz/¼ cup) hot coffee

For the buttercream

100g (3½oz/scant ½ cup) unsalted butter, softened, plus extra for greasing
80g (2¾oz/½ cup plus 1 Tbsp) icing (confectioners') sugar
½ tsp vanilla bean paste
20g (¾oz/3 Tbsp) unsweetened cocoa powder
pinch of fine sea salt
40g (1½oz) dark chocolate, melted
1½ Tbsp boiling water

Preheat the oven to 170°C (150°C fan/ 325°F/gas mark 3). Grease a 12-cm (5-in) round cake pan and line with baking paper.

Add the flour, sugar, cocoa powder, baking powder, bicarbonate of soda and salt to a bowl and mix to combine. Set aside.

In a separate bowl or jug (pitcher), mix the egg, milk and oil. Pour the wet ingredients into the dry and stir to get a thick, smooth batter.

Stir in the hot coffee and then pour the batter into the prepared pan.

Bake for 30–35 minutes until the cake is risen and a skewer inserted into the middle comes out clean.

Let it cool in the pan for 5 minutes before turning it out onto a wire rack to cool completely.

To make the buttercream, add the butter, icing sugar and vanilla to a bowl and beat for 2–3 minutes until smooth and fluffy. Beat in the cocoa powder and salt for another minute before pouring in the melted chocolate and beating until smooth. Stir in the boiling water; the mixture should be smooth and silky.

Split the cake into two horizontally and place the bottom layer on a piece of baking paper a couple of inches larger than the cake. This will help you lift and move it around when needed. Sandwich with a third of the buttercream, then add the rest to the top and sides of the cake. You can smooth it out with a palette knife or bench scraper, or go more rustic and add texture.

MAKE AHEAD

Make the cake and buttercream up to 2 days in advance.

sage & white chocolate madeleines

MAKE AHEAD

Make the batter the night before. The madeleines are best served on the day they are made.

Madeleines are such sweet little cakes that sound and look much more fancy than they are. I love bringing these for a relaxed evening dinner where we can have them with a late coffee or nightcap. If you know me and my recipe style, you know how much I enjoy adding fresh herbs to bakes where I can, and the sage leaves are right at home here. I know buying a whole new baking pan just for one recipe isn't always ideal, so you could make these in a mini-muffin pan. They just won't have the traditional shell pattern, but that is more than okay.

Makes 9

100g (3½oz/scant ½ cup) salted butter, plus extra for greasing
6 fresh sage leaves
2 eggs
90g (3¼oz/scant ½ cup) caster (superfine) sugar
10g (⅓oz/½ Tbsp) honey
110g (3¾oz/generous ¾ cup) plain (all-purpose) flour, plus extra for dusting
½ tsp baking powder
100g (3½oz) white chocolate

Add the butter to a small pan along with the sage leaves. Gently melt the butter and bring it to the boil before removing from the heat. Let the sage infuse for 10–20 minutes.

In a large bowl, whip the eggs, sugar and honey for a few minutes until thickened and pale. Fold in the flour and baking powder before gently folding in the strained cooled butter.

Cover the bowl with plastic wrap and chill in the fridge for at least 3 hours or overnight.

When you're ready to bake, grease your madeleine tray with butter, making sure to get in all the crevices. Dust lightly with a bit of flour and place in the fridge to chill for 30 minutes.

Preheat the oven to 200°C (180°C fan/ 400°F/gas mark 6). Spoon the batter evenly into the tray holes and bake the madeleines for 12–15 minutes until golden.

Remove from the oven and let them cool for 5 minutes before slipping them out of the tray and onto a wire rack to cool.

Wash and dry the madeleine tray and melt the white chocolate in the microwave or in a bowl set over a pan of simmering water.

Spoon about ½ a tablespoon of white chocolate into each madeleine hole and gently press a madeleine into each hole. Let the chocolate cool and firm up at room temperature for 30 minutes before moving to the fridge for another 30 minutes, or until you can pop the madeleines out the tray easily. Trim off any excess white chocolate using a sharp knife before serving.

crispy chocolate & dulce de leche tart

Everyone needs a few good no-bake recipes up their sleeve, and this is a fun one that reminds me of those krispie cakes you'd make as a child. All that's required here is some melting, mixing and chilling, so even if the thought of baking still intimidates you, this is a lovely place to start.

Serves 12

For the base
80g (2¾oz) dark chocolate
20g (1½ Tbsp) unsalted butter
65g (2¼oz) cocoa pop cereal
pinch of fine sea salt

For the filling
200g (7oz) dulce de leche
100g (3½oz) milk chocolate, finely chopped
100g (3½oz) dark chocolate, finely chopped
220ml (7½fl oz/scant 1 cup) double (heavy) cream
2 small cinnamon sticks

To finish
flaky sea salt
caramelized cereal crunch (page 182), optional

To make the base, add the chocolate and butter to a heatproof bowl and place over a pan of simmering water. Stir gently until melted. Alternatively, melt in short bursts in the microwave.

Tip in the cereal and salt and give it a good stir until coated. Spoon into a 20-cm (8-in) round loose-bottomed cake pan and use the back of a spoon to press it down.

Chill the base in the fridge for 20 minutes or until firm. Once chilled, spoon and spread your dulce de leche on top of the base, leaving about a 5-mm (¼-in) border around the edges. Place it back in the fridge while you make your ganache.

Add all the chopped chocolate to a bowl. Put the cream and cinnamon sticks in a small saucepan and heat until steaming but not boiling. (If you have time, remove from the heat and let the cinnamon infuse in the cream for 15 minutes, then remove the cinnamon sticks and reheat the cream until hot again.) Pour the hot cream over the chocolate and let it sit for 30 seconds.

Slowly stir the ganache until smooth and silky. If there are still some unmelted bits of chocolate, place the bowl over a pan of simmering water and let it heat gently until melted.

Pour the ganache on top of the dulce de leche layer and chill in the fridge for 2–3 hours or until fully set.

Top with flaky sea salt and some caramelized cereal crunch, if using.
To get clean slices when serving, dip a sharp knife in hot water before slicing.

MAKE AHEAD

Make up to 1 day ahead; any longer and the base will start to soften.

clotted cream chocolate chip cake

MAKE AHEAD

Best served on the day it's made.

Clotted cream has cemented itself as the ultimate accompaniment to a scone but it can be used for so many more things! In a cake, it works wonders to create something rich and creamy with the softest crumb. It's a little unassuming but feels really comforting and homely. A good one to bring to a coffee morning or weekend brunch. I have to suggest serving this with an extra dollop of clotted cream because anything else would just be silly.

Serves 8

2 Tbsp neutral oil (such as sunflower or vegetable), plus extra for greasing
2 eggs
200g (7oz/1 cup) caster (superfine) sugar
½ Tbsp malt extract
225g (8oz/1 cup) clotted cream, plus extra to serve
175g (6oz/1⅓ cups) plain (all-purpose) flour, plus ½ tsp for the chocolate
1 tsp baking powder
¼ tsp fine sea salt
100g (3½oz) milk chocolate, roughly chopped
1 tsp demerara (turbinado) sugar

Preheat the oven to 180°C (160°C fan/350°F/gas mark 4). Grease a 20-cm (8-in) round cake pan and line with baking paper.

Add the eggs, caster sugar and malt extract to a large bowl, or the bowl of a stand mixer, and whisk (using an electric whisk if not using a stand mixer) to whip the eggs on a medium-high speed for 2–3 minutes, until thick and pale.

Stir the clotted cream to loosen it up and then fold this into the egg mixture, being careful not to knock out too much air.

In a separate bowl, mix together the flour, baking powder and salt. Add this to the egg mixture in 3 batches, carefully folding it in until smooth.

Reserve 1 tablespoon of the chopped chocolate and toss the rest in the ½ teaspoon of flour to coat, then fold this into the batter. Mix the reserved chopped chocolate with the demerara sugar.

Pour the batter into the prepared pan, sprinkle over the demerara and chocolate mixture and bake for 45–50 minutes until well risen and a skewer inserted into the middle comes out clean.

Let it cool completely before serving with a dollop of clotted cream.

chocolate, banana & cardamom cream pie

This dessert is slightly inspired by a banoffee pie. I've always found it way too sweet and hankered after a banana dessert that was a little more up my street. Introducing chocolate into the mix helped balance things out while still feeling a bit playful.

Serves 10

For the base
170g (6oz) digestive biscuits (graham crackers)
30g (1oz/2½ Tbsp) caster (superfine) sugar
60g (2¼oz/¼ cup) unsalted butter, melted

For the filling
4 egg yolks
80g (2¾oz/generous ⅓ cup) caster (superfine) sugar
1½ tsp unsweetened cocoa powder
20g (¾oz/2 Tbsp) cornflour (cornstarch)
400ml (14fl oz/1¾ cups) milk
½ tsp ground cardamom
¼ tsp fine sea salt
50g (1¾oz) dark chocolate, finely chopped
40g (1½oz) milk chocolate, finely chopped
20g (1½ Tbsp) unsalted butter, at room temperature
3 small ripe bananas, sliced

To finish
300ml (12fl oz/1½ cups) double (heavy) cream
1 tsp vanilla bean paste
handful of dark chocolate shavings

Preheat the oven to 180°C (160°C fan/ 350°F/gas mark 4).

For the base, blitz the biscuits in a food processor or bash them up in a food bag. Mix in the sugar and stir in the melted butter until the biscuits are fully coated.

Press the crushed biscuits firmly into a 23-cm (9-in) round pie dish and bake the base for 15 minutes. Remove from the oven and let it cool completely.

To make the filling, add the egg yolks and half of the sugar to a bowl and whisk until smooth. Stir in the cocoa powder and cornflour and set aside.

Add the milk, the rest of the sugar, the cardamom and salt to a saucepan and heat until steaming, but don't let it come to the boil. Pour a third of the hot milk onto the eggs and whisk to combine. Slowly pour in the rest of the milk and then tip everything back into the saucepan.

Gently heat the custard while stirring constantly; after 2–3 minutes, it'll start to thicken. Once the custard starts bubbling, keep whisking for another 30 seconds and then remove from the heat. Pour the custard into a clean bowl and tip in all the chopped chocolate. Stir it in until melted, before mixing in the butter.

Cover with some plastic wrap, making sure it is touching the surface, and let the custard cool to room temperature. Place in the fridge for 3–4 hours until well chilled.

When you're ready to assemble, give the chocolate custard a whisk until smooth. Add a thin layer onto the biscuit crust and top with a layer of sliced bananas. Spoon on the rest of the chocolate custard and top with the remaining bananas.

To finish, lightly whip the cream with the vanilla and spoon on top of the pie. Sprinkle on some chocolate shavings and chill until ready to serve.

MAKE AHEAD

Make up to 1 day in advance.

something creamy

This chapter feels, in many ways, a love letter to custard. It's truly one of my favourite things, be it hot, cold, baked, brûléed, runny or filled in a doughnut. I could go on and on. This chapter contains a lot of the big classics – I'm talking cheesecakes, tiramisu, and pavlovas; all the things that come to mind when you think of dessert. So enjoy working your way through these recipes; no matter what you decide to bring, it'll be a winner.

miso & nutmeg custard pie

MAKE AHEAD

Bake the pastry case 2 days in advance, then continue and bake the filling on the day you want to serve.

Make this for all the custard lovers in your life and they'll love you forever. It's the perfect balance of sweet and salty and one of my absolute favourites.

Serves 12

For the crust

190g (6¾oz/scant 1½ cups) plain (all-purpose) flour, plus extra for dusting
1 Tbsp caster (superfine) sugar
¼ tsp fine sea salt
125g (4½oz/½ cup plus 1 Tbsp) cold unsalted butter, diced
80–90ml (5–6 Tbsp) cold water

For the filling

1 egg, plus 4 egg yolks
70g (2½oz/generous ⅓ cup) light brown sugar
300ml (10½fl oz/generous 1¼ cups) milk
200ml double (heavy) cream
40g (1½oz) white miso
50g (1¾oz/¼ cup) caster (superfine) sugar
1 tsp vanilla bean paste
freshly grated nutmeg

To make the crust, add the flour, sugar and salt to a bowl. Add the diced butter and toss to coat in the flour. Use your fingertips to rub the butter into the flour until you have a coarse mixture with small chunks of butter. Make a well in the centre and pour in 60ml (4 Tbsp) water. Stir to start bringing it together and continue to add water a tablespoon at a time until you have a rough dough.

Turn it out onto a floured surface, and gently fold it over itself a couple of times to bring it together. Pat it into a thick disc, wrap in plastic wrap and chill in the fridge for 2–3 hours.

Lightly flour your work surface and roll out the dough about 2.5cm (1in) wider than your 23-cm (9-in) pie dish. Gently roll the pastry over your rolling pin and then lift and unroll it into your dish. Make sure the pastry is completely flush against the edges of the dish, then tuck the edges underneath itself to sit on the rim. Crimp the edges with your fingers. Chill in the freezer for 15 minutes.

Preheat the oven to 220°C (200°C fan/ 425°F/gas mark 7).

Dock the base of the pastry all over with a fork. Line with baking paper and then fill with baking beans or uncooked rice. Bake for 15 minutes before removing the baking paper and beans and baking for a further 10 minutes until the edges are golden and the base looks dry.

Remove from the oven and set aside to cool. Reduce the oven temperature to 150°C (130°C fan/300°F/gas mark 2).

For the filling, add the whole egg, yolks, and sugar to a bowl. Mix to combine and set aside. Add the milk, cream, miso, caster sugar and vanilla to a small saucepan. Heat gently until the miso dissolves and the milk is hot but not boiling.

Pour the milk over the eggs in 3 batches, whisking continuously to combine. Strain the custard and let it sit for a minute – skimming off any foam that rises to the top – then pour into the pie crust. Sprinkle some grated nutmeg all over the surface and bake for 25–30 minutes or until the custard is set around the edges but still has a little jiggle in the middle.

Let the pie cool completely before slicing and eating at room temperature. Or wrap and chill in the fridge to store.

burnt Basque cheesecake

If you've been anywhere near social media over the past few years, it's highly likely you'll have come across a burnt Basque cheesecake and all of its bronzed-top glory. It's a bit iconic, the deeply browned surface, the squidgy folds from the baking paper and the soft, creamy, sometimes oozy interior. It's a deceptively simple bake with few ingredients and a pretty straightforward method, but when done right is just pure joy. Eat it when still warm for a soft set, slightly jiggly consistency, or after a night in the fridge it firms up a little, giving something that's easier to slice.

A hot oven is super-important here to get that signature dark surface, but not many bakes highlight the disparity between ovens as much as this. Give your oven plenty of time to preheat; sometimes mine comes out a bit lighter on top but I'd prefer that than keeping it in too long and overbaking.

Serves 12

750g (1lb 10½oz/3⅓ cups) full-fat cream cheese
220g (7¾oz/generous 1 cup) caster (superfine) sugar
3 large eggs, plus 2 egg yolks
300ml (10½fl oz/generous 1¼ cups) double (heavy) cream
1 tsp fine sea salt
20g (¾oz/2½ Tbsp) plain (all-purpose) flour

Preheat the oven to 240°C (220°C fan/ 475°F/gas mark 9). Scrunch and then unscrunch 2 large sheets of baking paper and use them to line a deep round 20-cm (8-in) cake pan. Make sure there's enough paper to overhang over the edges and that the paper is pressed well into the edges.

Add the cream cheese and sugar to the bowl of a stand mixer and beat on low speed until smooth. Add in the whole eggs one by one followed by the yolks, and then mix in the cream and salt.

Take out about 100ml (3½fl oz/ scant ½ cup) of the batter and add it to a small bowl. Add in the flour and mix until smooth before adding this back into your main mixture.

Pour the batter into your prepared pan and bake for 40–45 minutes. The cheesecake will be well risen with a dark surface but still very jiggly with a big wobble – it's a much bigger jiggle than you normally have with other cheesecakes and custards.

Remove from the oven and leave to cool for 2 hours or until it reaches room temperature. It'll sink a little bit but that's totally fine and expected! You can serve as is, or chill in the fridge for a few hours, which allows you to get neat slices.

MAKE AHEAD

Make up to 3 days in advance. Store well wrapped in the fridge.

salted honey sesame tart

MAKE AHEAD

Make the tart up to 1 day ahead and store in the fridge.

This delicate tart feels fancy yet homely at the same time. The buttery base holds a salted, honey-scented custard that melts in the mouth. Try to use a rich, fragrant honey if you can for the best flavour. If there's one thing I don't want you to skip, it's the sesame crunch sprinkled liberally on top. It just ties everything together and brings a little more savouriness and texture.

Serves 10–12

For the pastry

200g (7oz/1½ cups) plain (all-purpose) flour, plus extra for dusting
95g (3⅓oz/⅓ cup plus 1 Tbsp) cold unsalted butter, diced
40g (1½oz/4½ Tbsp) icing (confectioners') sugar
pinch of fine sea salt
1 large egg, separated
1 Tbsp cold water

For the filling

1 large egg, plus 6 large egg yolks
600ml (20fl oz/2½ cups) whipping (heavy) cream
150g (5½oz/generous ½ cup) honey
½ tsp flaky sea salt

To finish and serve

crème fraîche
2 Tbsp sesame crunch (page 187)

Put the flour, butter, icing sugar and salt in a food processor and blitz until fine. Add the egg yolk and cold water, then pulse until it forms a ball; if the dough seems dry, add another tablespoon of water. Bring together on a lightly floured surface, wrap and chill for 2–3 hours, until firm.

Preheat the oven to 190°C (170°C fan/375°F/gas mark 5).

On a floured surface, roll the pastry to 2–3mm (⅛in) thick and use it to line a 23-cm (9-in) fluted tart pan. Prick all over with a fork, line with a scrunched-up piece of baking paper and fill with baking beans or uncooked rice. Blind bake for 20 minutes, then lift out the paper and beans and bake for 15 minutes more, until lightly browned. Brush the base with a little egg white and bake again for a minute to seal.

Turn the oven temperature down to 120°C (110°C fan/250°F/gas mark ½).

To make the filling, whisk the egg and egg yolks in a large bowl. Put the cream and honey in a saucepan, heat gently until steaming, then add the salt and slowly whisk into the egg mix. Don't whisk too vigorously here or you'll create lots of air bubbles. Leave to sit for a few minutes, then skim off any foam. Pour the custard through a fine sieve (strainer) into a jug (pitcher).

Put the tart case on an oven tray and pour in half the custard. Transfer to the oven, then pour in the rest of the custard. Bake for 40–45 minutes, until the edges of the filling are set but still a little wobbly in the middle. Remove from the oven and leave to cool completely.

You can serve this at room temperature or chilled from the fridge. Right before serving, top with dollops of crème fraîche and sprinkle over some sesame crunch.

milky tea tres leches

MAKE AHEAD

Make up to 2 days in advance and store in the fridge.

This is inspired by a Hong Kong milk tea which is delightfully creamy, sweet and refreshing. All of the best creamy things (condensed milk, evaporated milk and full-fat milk) come together to generously soak the light sponge. A tres leches cake is ideal for making ahead as it benefits from an overnight chill in the fridge. The malty, slightly bitter notes from the tea helps to avoid this being sickly and a bit of lightly whipped cream tops it all off.

Serves 9–12

butter, for greasing
3 eggs
130g (4¾oz/⅔ cup) golden caster (superfine) sugar
40g (1½oz/3¼ Tbsp) light brown sugar
1 tsp vanilla bean paste
140g (5oz/generous 1 cup) plain (all-purpose) flour
½ tsp fine sea salt
1 tsp baking powder
100ml (3½fl oz/scant ½ cup) milk
250ml (9fl oz/generous 1 cup) double (heavy) cream, to serve

For the soak

250ml (9fl oz/generous 1 cup) milk
250ml (9fl oz/generous 1 cup) evaporated milk
5 Ceylon or English breakfast tea bags
1 x 397g (14oz) can of condensed milk

To make the soak, add the milk and evaporated milk to a small saucepan. Gently heat and then add in the tea bags. Brew over a low heat for 2–3 minutes, giving it a mix every now and again. Remove from the heat, cover and let it steep for 20 minutes or until cool. Strain the mixture into a jug (pitcher) and discard the tea bags. Mix in the condensed milk and set aside until later.

Preheat the oven to 190°C (170°C fan/375°F/gas mark 5). Grease a 20-cm (8-in) square baking pan and line with baking paper, leaving enough overhang to help you lift it out later.

In the bowl of a stand mixer or a large bowl using an electric whisk, whip the eggs, both sugars and the vanilla for 3–4 minutes on high speed until the mixture is thick, airy and pale.

In a separate bowl, mix together the flour, salt and baking powder. Add half of this to the egg mixture and gently fold with a spatula until combined. Pour in the milk and gently mix, then fold in the rest of the flour before pouring the batter into the prepared baking pan.

Bake for 30–35 minutes until the cake is well browned and a skewer inserted into the middle comes out clean.

Let it cool for 10 minutes before using a skewer to poke holes across the cake. Gradually pour the milky tea over the cake, letting it soak in before adding more. Let the cake cool to room temperature before covering and chilling in the fridge for at least 6 hours but ideally overnight.

Whip the cream in a small bowl until you have soft peaks. Spoon and swirl it on top of the cake before slicing up to serve.

no-bake sweet & salty cheesecake

MAKE AHEAD

Make up to 1 day in advance (any longer and the crackers start to soften too much).

Heavily and shamelessly inspired by one of my favourite places in London to get a Sunday roast: Blacklock. A visit here is never complete without their iconic white chocolate cheesecake that gets very generously scooped from its dish straight into your bowl at the table. It's the informality and homely vibe of it that I love and have recreated here. The biscuits are kept quite chunky and the topping is just sweet enough. I've gone for Ritz crackers for saltiness and condensed milk because it's one of the best things that comes in a can.

Serves 6

260g (9¼oz) Ritz crackers
135g (4¾oz/⅔ cup minus 1 Tbsp) salted butter, melted
390g (13¾oz/1¾ cups) cream cheese
150g (5½oz/⅔ cup) sour cream
3 tsp vanilla bean paste
340ml (11½fl oz/scant 1½ cups) condensed milk, plus extra to drizzle
300ml (10½fl oz/generous 1¼ cups) double (heavy) cream
flaky sea salt, to serve

Add the crackers to a bowl and bash with a rolling pin until mostly broken up. You want a rough mix of smaller and larger pieces.

Pour in the melted butter and stir to coat. Add the coated crackers to a small serving dish and chill in the fridge while you make the filling.

Add the cream cheese, sour cream and vanilla to a bowl and mix until smooth. Stir in the condensed milk.

In a separate bowl, lightly whip the cream until you have very soft peaks. Fold this into the cream cheese mixture and then spoon everything into the dish on top of the crackers.

Chill in the fridge for 3–4 hours. When you're ready to serve, drizzle with a little extra condensed milk and a little flaky sea salt. Scoop generously into bowls to serve.

creamy coconut & passionfruit tart

This is a refreshing, summery pudding that works well when bringing something for a group with dietary requirements. It's already vegan but it's easy to make gluten-free by switching up the biscuits in the base if needed. I love eating this cold straight from the fridge. It's rich with coconut and brightened up with passionfruit. Make sure the coconut cream is properly chilled so it whips up enough to fold into the filling.

Serves 8–12

For the crust

- 25g (1oz) desiccated (grated unsweetened) coconut
- 150g (5½oz) gingersnap biscuits/cookies (ensure vegan if needed)
- 90g (3¼oz/⅓ cup plus 1 Tbsp) coconut oil, melted

For the filling

- 30g (1oz/3 Tbsp) cornflour (cornstarch)
- 120ml (4fl oz/½ cup) oat milk
- 1 x 400ml (14fl oz/1¾ cups) can of full-fat coconut milk
- 100g (3½oz/½ cup) caster (superfine) sugar
- 1 tsp vanilla bean paste
- 250g (9oz/generous 1 cup) coconut cream, well chilled

For the topping

- 2 passionfruit
- 1 Tbsp caster (superfine) sugar

To make the crust, add the desiccated coconut to a small frying pan and toast for 1–2 minutes until lightly browned and fragrant.

Add the gingersnaps to a food processor and blitz until fine. Pour into a bowl and mix in the toasted coconut. Stir in the melted coconut oil and mix until the biscuits are well coated. Pour the mixture into a 23-cm (9-in) fluted tart pan, pressing it in firmly and evenly. Place in the fridge to chill while you make the filling.

Add the cornflour to a saucepan with 2–3 tablespoons of the oat milk. Mix until you have a smooth consistency. Add in the rest of the oat milk, the coconut milk, sugar and vanilla. Heat gently, while stirring frequently until the mixture thickens. Once it starts bubbling, remove from the heat and pour into a clean bowl.

Cover with plastic wrap that touches the surface and set aside to cool to room temperature. Place in the fridge to chill completely. Once chilled, give it a good whisk by hand to remove any lumps.

Add your coconut cream to a bowl and whip with an electric whisk until light and fluffy. Fold this into your coconut mixture and pour the whole thing onto the biscuit base.

Chill in the fridge for 4 hours until set.

To make the topping, add the passionfruit pulp and sugar to a small saucepan and heat until the sugar dissolves and looks syrupy. Let it cool completely before spooning it on top of the tart.

MAKE AHEAD

Make the tart up to 1 day ahead; any longer and the biscuit base will soften too much.

brown sugar & burnt butter rice pudding

MAKE AHEAD

Make up to 2 days ahead and store, covered with plastic wrap, in the fridge. Reheat as directed above.

I know rice pudding isn't for everyone, but it most certainly is for me. Knowing it can be a little divisive, I wouldn't necessarily bring this dessert to a large group gathering where a crowd pleaser might be a better option. I find this works much better for smaller, more intimate or casual settings where you can easily gauge what the vibe is towards slow-cooked, creamy rice.

I prefer mine cold from the fridge with a little extra milk stirred in to loosen before serving. Some crunchy demerara on top adds just enough texture to an otherwise very soft pudding, but if you need a little more, you can serve with the tuiles or caramelized cereal crunch on pages 185 and 182.

Serves 4–6

60g (2¼oz/¼ cup) unsalted butter
60g (2¼oz/5 Tbsp) light muscovado sugar
80g (2¾oz/scant ½ cup) short-grain pudding rice
700ml (23½fl oz/3 cups) milk, plus extra to serve
250ml (9fl oz/generous 1 cup) double (heavy) cream
¼ tsp fine sea salt
demerara (turbinado) sugar, to serve (optional)

Add the butter to a large saucepan and heat gently to melt. Continue cooking the butter until it starts to get foamy. Once it starts smelling fragrant and begins to brown, quickly tip in the muscovado sugar and stir to combine. Add in the rice and mix for 1–2 minutes until properly coated and toasty.

Pour in the milk, cream and salt. Bring to the boil and then reduce the heat to low. Stir frequently to make sure the rice doesn't stick; it'll take about 45–60 minutes until the rice is tender and thickened.

You can serve the rice pudding straight away or pour into a clean container and cover with some plastic wrap touching the surface until completely cool. Chill in the fridge and then stir in some extra milk or cream to loosen before serving cold. To reheat, add the rice pudding to a pan with a good splash of milk and heat gently until steaming. Top with demerara sugar, if you like.

tiramisu

A dessert book without a recipe for tiramisu wouldn't be a very good dessert book at all. This may just be my favourite dessert of all time and is by far one of my most made when I've been asked to bring something. Now, there are hundreds and thousands of tiramisu recipes available and mine isn't necessarily super traditional, but it's exactly how I love it. Rich, almost custard-like mascarpone, a good hit of coffee, just enough alcohol to know it's there but not to overpower, and a very generous dusting of cocoa powder to finish.

This isn't a last-minute dessert, so a bit of forward planning is a must. It needs time to sit overnight for everything to settle and mingle together. It should be just soft enough to scoop and spoon into bowls, barely holding its own weight but not sloppy. Never sloppy. I could go on and on about this one but if you need to bring dessert and are not sure where to start, this will always be a winner.

Serves 10–12

5 egg yolks
80g (2¾oz/generous ⅓ cup) caster (superfine) sugar
500g (1lb 2oz/2¼ cups) mascarpone
250ml (9fl oz/generous 1 cup) double (heavy) cream
60ml (2fl oz/¼ cup) sweet Marsala or dark rum
350ml (12fl oz/1½ cups) strong brewed coffee
90ml (6 Tbsp) coffee liqueur
26 savoiardi biscuits or lady fingers
unsweetened cocoa powder, to finish

Add the egg yolks and sugar to a large bowl and whisk on medium-high speed for about 2 minutes until they are thick and pale.

Add in the mascarpone in 4 batches, whisking well after each addition and making sure you don't have any lumps.

In a separate bowl, lightly whip the cream until you just have soft peaks. Gently fold this into the egg mixture to combine. Fold in the Marsala and set aside until needed.

Add your coffee to a large, shallow dish and stir in the coffee liqueur. Dip the savoiardi biscuits in one at time – make sure both sides get a dip in the coffee but be fairly quick. If you leave them any longer than about 5 seconds they'll start to fall apart.

Arrange a layer of the soaked biscuits on the bottom of your dish. You may have to break some in half to fill in any gaps. Spoon half of the mascarpone mixture on top and smooth it out with a palette knife.

Repeat with another layer of soaked biscuits and then top with the remaining mascarpone, smoothing the surface. Lightly cover with some plastic wrap and chill in the fridge overnight. If you don't have that long, then let it chill for at least 6 hours, but overnight is best.

When you're ready to serve, dust the top of the tiramisu well with cocoa powder and spoon generous servings into bowls.

MAKE AHEAD

Definitely! Make at least 1 day ahead and up to 2. Store in the fridge as directed in the recipe.

vegan pavlovas

MAKE AHEAD

Make the meringue shells 1 day in advance and store in an airtight container.

The liquid in a can of chickpeas, properly known as aquafaba, is a bit of a magical ingredient. Particularly in vegan baking. For a while, I was quite hesitant to use it, fearing everything I made would taste like chickpeas. Spoiler – it doesn't! The aquafaba whips up beautifully to create an egg-free meringue that once you're comfortable with, you can fill with pretty much anything you fancy. Make them bigger or smaller, pile them up on a platter for something dramatic or crush them into an Eton mess. I've gone for a ginger, nectarine and almond pavlova that is simply beautiful for a cosy summer evening dessert.

Serves 6

For the meringue

liquid (aquafaba) from 1 x 400g (14oz) can of chickpeas
1 tsp lemon juice or white wine vinegar
240g (8½oz/1¼ cups) caster (superfine) sugar
1 tsp cornflour (cornstarch)

Preheat the oven to 160°C (140°C fan/325°F/gas mark 3). Line a large baking tray with baking paper.

Add the aquafaba to the bowl of a stand mixer with the lemon juice or vinegar and mix on low speed for about a minute. Increase the speed to medium-high and continue whisking until the mixture looks white and frothy with very soft peaks.

With the mixer still running, start adding in the sugar about a tablespoon at a time, waiting 20 seconds before adding in the next batch. Once all the sugar has been added, keep mixing for another minute and you should have a thick, glossy mixture. Add in the cornflour and mix briefly to combine.

Spoon 6 dollops onto the baking tray and use a palette knife or the back of a spoon to smooth the edges and shape them into mounds. Use a hot spoon to make an indent in the middle. This will be where our filling will sit later.

Bake the pavlovas for 45–55 minutes or until they are dry to the touch and peel away from the paper easily. Turn the oven off and leave them to cool and dry out inside the oven for 3 hours before storing them in an airtight container until needed.

continued overleaf

vegan pavlovas continued

To fill

3 ripe nectarines, pitted and quartered
2 Tbsp maple syrup
juice of ½ lemon
1 Tbsp Amaretto (optional)
1 Tbsp finely chopped stem ginger
350ml (12fl oz/1½ cups) plant-based double (heavy) cream
1 tsp vanilla bean paste

For the almonds

40g (1½oz/½ cup) flaked (slivered) almonds
½ Tbsp maple syrup
½ Tbsp icing (confectioners') sugar
pinch of flaky sea salt

For the nectarines, preheat the oven to 210°C (190°C fan/410°F/gas mark 7). Add the nectarines to a small dish with the maple syrup, lemon juice and Amaretto, if using. Bake in the oven for 15 minutes until the fruit is softened and syrupy. Remove from the oven, and when cool enough to handle, peel off the skins. Stir in the chopped stem ginger and leave to cool completely.

To make the almonds, add them to a lined baking tray, pour over the maple syrup and dust with the icing sugar. Mix to coat and then bake in the oven for 12–15 minutes until toasty and well browned. Sprinkle with the flaky sea salt and let them cool completely before breaking into smaller pieces.

Lightly whip the cream and vanilla until thickened, then, when you're ready to serve, fill each meringue shell with the cream. Top with some nectarines, a little of the syrup and a sprinkling of the toasted flaked almonds.

pavlova

The mother of all desserts. One of my most made, most reliable crowd pleasers is a big fat pavlova. It can do all things. Make it as over-the-top or as understated as you fancy. Bake it in layers, go for a big nest to fill to the brim with cream and fruit, pipe it into a wreath at Christmas, or make them smaller, individually sized to avoid arguments. The choice is all yours. I like mine as one big mass. Crisp, sugary edges holding together a soft marshmallow middle, waiting to be piled with clouds of cream. Bake it the day before and let it dry out in the oven overnight. Transporting an assembled pavlova is risky business so I'll usually take all my prepped fruit and whip some cream when I'm at my destination.

Serves 10–12

For the meringue
160g (5¾oz) egg whites (from 4 large eggs)
1 tsp lemon juice or white wine vinegar
280g (10oz/scant 1½ cups) caster (superfine) sugar
½ Tbsp cornflour (cornstarch)

To fill
600ml (20fl oz/2½ cups) double (heavy) cream
½ Tbsp icing (confectioners') sugar
1½ tsp vanilla bean paste
your choice of fruits: anything from passionfruit, berries, mangoes, peaches etc.

Preheat the oven to 120°C (110°C fan/ 250°F/gas mark ½). Line a large baking tray with baking paper.

Add the egg whites and lemon juice or vinegar to the bowl of a stand mixer with the whisk attachment.

Start whisking on medium-high speed until the egg whites start getting foamy. Once they get to soft peaks, start adding your sugar 2 tablespoons at a time, waiting for it to incorporate properly before adding the next batch.

Once all the sugar has been added, continue whipping the meringue for a further 5 minutes. It'll feel like a long time but it's important to help the sugar dissolve. The meringue should be thick, stiff and glossy. Add in the cornflour and whisk briefly to combine.

Spoon the meringue onto the baking tray in one big mound. (To stop the baking paper sliding around, use a little of the meringue as 'glue' to stick it to the tray.) Use a palette knife to shape the meringue into a dome and then make a dip in the middle, where the filling will go later. You can leave the sides smooth or use a palette knife to add some texture.

Bake for 70–80 minutes or until the meringue looks dry to the touch and can easily lift off from the baking paper. Turn the oven off and let the pavlova cool inside completely, for at least 3 hours but ideally overnight.

When you're ready to fill, lightly whip the cream, sugar and vanilla until you just get to soft peaks. Prepare whatever fruit you've chosen and pile it all in the middle of the pavlova. Once assembled, serve within a few hours.

MAKE AHEAD

Make the meringue base up to 2 days ahead and store in an airtight container. Fill with cream and fruit just before serving.

malty cream puff tumble

Cream puffs are a bit retro, but in the best way. My earliest memories of them involve supermarket versions which would be cold and dry with overwhipped cream, but I still loved them. The best bit was, and still is, warming up the chocolate sauce to pour on top. I like to do this at the table – this is a dessert that calls for as much drama as possible. Pile the cream puffs high on a platter and generously douse them in sauce. I'll add a good sprinkle of toasty hazelnuts to finish and maybe even a sparkler or two if I'm feeling extra theatrical.

Serves 8

For the cream puffs
90ml (3fl oz/6 Tbsp) water
90ml (3fl oz/6 Tbsp) milk
75g (2½oz/⅓ cup) salted butter
2 tsp caster (superfine) sugar
120g (4¼oz/scant 1 cup) plain (all-purpose) flour
3 eggs, beaten

Preheat the oven to 180°C (160°C fan/350°F/gas mark 4). Line a large baking tray with baking paper.

Add the water, milk, butter and sugar to a small saucepan and bring to the boil. Tip in the flour all at once and mix quickly to get a thick dough. It will be lumpy at first but will eventually come together. Keep cooking and mixing the dough for about a minute to cook out the flour and then transfer it to a clean bowl to cool down a little.

Add the beaten eggs a little bit at a time, mixing well before adding some more. You can mix by hand or with an electric whisk. It will look lumpy and split at first but keep going and it will come together. Keep adding the egg until you have a glossy mixture that is still thick but drops slowly from the spoon – you may not need to add all the egg.

Spoon the dough into a piping (pastry) bag and snip off the end. Pipe blobs of choux pastry about 2.5cm (1in) wide, leaving about a 1-cm (½-in) gap between them. Gently brush the tops with any remaining beaten egg and bake for 25–30 minutes until they are well risen and deeply browned.

Once baked, use a skewer to pierce the bottoms to allow steam to escape and place them upside down. Let them cool for 20 minutes in the oven to dry out a bit.

MAKE AHEAD

Make the cream puff shells up to 2 days ahead and store in an airtight container. Crisp them up again in the oven for 5–10 minutes and let them cool before filling.

continued overleaf

malty cream puff tumble continued

For the filling
400ml (14fl oz/1¾ cups) double (heavy) cream
70g malted milk powder (such as Horlicks; not instant)
1 tsp vanilla bean paste
1 Tbsp icing (confectioners') sugar
1 Tbsp milk

For the chocolate sauce
150g (5½oz) dark chocolate, roughly chopped
250ml (9fl oz/generous 1 cup) water
80g (2¾oz/generous ⅓ cup) light brown sugar
½ tsp flaky sea salt
50ml (2fl oz/3½ Tbsp) double (heavy) cream

To finish
handful of toasted hazelnuts, chopped

To make the filling, add the cream, malted milk powder, vanilla, icing sugar and milk to a bowl. Give it a mix to help the powder start dissolving and then whisk until you have soft peaks. Set aside in the fridge to chill until needed.

To make the chocolate sauce, add everything except the cream to a small saucepan and heat gently to melt the chocolate. Bring to the boil and stir frequently. After 2–3 minutes or so the chocolate will thicken and become smooth. Remove from the heat and stir in the cream. Set aside to cool a little.

Split the cooled cream puffs in half, not quite cutting all the way through, and fill with some of the malted cream.

When you're ready to serve, pile up the filled cream puffs on a platter. Pour the chocolate sauce on top and sprinkle with chopped hazelnuts.

tahini, sumac & strawberry trifle

The beauty of a trifle is that it can be anything you want it to be. I've never been a fan of jelly (jello) in a trifle, so I just leave it out. And I prefer making mine in a shallow dish – those traditional, deep trifle bowls are visually stunning but a pain to travel with and most people, including myself, don't actually own one. If I'm bringing a trifle for dessert, I'll assemble the cake, fruit and custard layer together in advance and then just top with fresh cream and any extras right before serving.

Serves 10–12

For the tahini sponge
120g (4¼oz/½ cup) unsalted butter, melted
180g (6¼oz/scant 1 cup) light brown sugar
70g (2½oz/⅓ cup) tahini
1 tsp vanilla bean paste
2 eggs
180g (6¼oz/1⅓ cups) plain (all-purpose) flour
2 tsp baking powder
¼ tsp fine sea salt
80ml (2½fl oz/⅓ cup) milk

For the custard
5 egg yolks
80g (2¾oz/generous ⅓ cup) caster (superfine) sugar
25g (1oz/scant ¼ cup) cornflour (cornstarch)
350ml (12fl oz/1½ cups) milk
150ml (5fl oz/scant ⅔ cup) double (heavy) cream
1 tsp vanilla bean paste
50g (1¾oz) white chocolate, roughly chopped

Preheat the oven to 180°C (160°C fan/ 350°F/gas mark 4). Grease a 20-cm (8-in) square baking pan and line with baking paper.

Add the melted butter, sugar, tahini and vanilla to a bowl and mix to combine. Mix in the eggs. Stir in the flour, baking powder and salt until smooth before mixing in the milk. Pour the batter into the tin and bake for 25–28 minutes or until the cake is well browned and a skewer inserted into the centre comes out clean. Set aside to cool completely.

To make the custard, add the yolks, half of the sugar and the cornflour to a bowl and whisk until smooth.

Heat the milk, cream, vanilla and remaining sugar in a small saucepan until steaming and then pour a quarter of it onto the eggs. Give it a good whisk to combine while slowly pouring in the rest of the hot milk.

Pour everything back into the saucepan and heat gently while stirring continuously. The custard will begin to thicken after about 4–5 minutes. Once it looks thickened and starts bubbling, remove from the heat and pour it through a sieve (strainer) into a clean, shallow bowl. Stir in the white chocolate until melted and then cover with a piece of plastic wrap, so it is touching the surface. Set aside to cool completely before chilling in the fridge until needed. Before using, give it a good mix with a whisk to remove any lumps.

continued overleaf

MAKE AHEAD

Make the individual elements up to 2 days ahead and assemble on the day.

tahini, sumac & strawberry trifle continued

For the strawberries
750g (1lb 10½oz) strawberries, hulled
3 tsp sumac
juice of ½ lemon
100g (3½oz/½ cup) caster (superfine) sugar
½ tsp rosewater

To finish
200ml (7fl oz/scant 1 cup) double (heavy) cream
2 Tbsp sesame crunch (page 187)

Add half the strawberries to a saucepan with the sumac, lemon juice and the sugar, keeping back 1 tablespoon of sugar. Let it come to the boil before reducing the heat and simmering for about 7–9 minutes until the strawberries have broken down and start to look jammy. Set aside to cool completely.

Slice the remaining strawberries and toss in the reserved 1 tablespoon of sugar and the rosewater, then set aside.

When you're ready to assemble, slice the cake into small cubes and arrange it in the bottom of a shallow glass or ceramic baking dish. Spoon the jam on top, spreading it out to cover the cake. Top with the sliced strawberries followed by the custard.

To finish, lightly whip the cream and stop as soon as you have soft peaks. Dollop the cream on top, finishing with a sprinkling of the sesame crunch.

spiced milk flan

MAKE AHEAD

Make up to 3 days ahead and store well wrapped in the fridge. Turn it out of the loaf pan when you're ready to serve.

There are many different ways to make a flan. Some are more dense, made with just the yolks, and others are more creamy and light with much more wobble. This leans more to the Mexican version which uses whole eggs and condensed milk but with added spices for something more fragrant. Don't be scared to take your caramel nice and dark; we want some of that sugary bitterness to balance out the richness.

Serves 8

350ml (12fl oz/1½ cups) milk
100ml (3½fl oz/scant ½ cup) double (heavy) cream
200g (7oz/⅔ cup) condensed milk
1 vanilla pod (bean), split lengthways, or 1 tsp vanilla bean paste
1 cinnamon stick
8 green cardamom pods, lightly bashed
30g (1oz) fresh ginger, thinly sliced
1 star anise
pinch of fine sea salt
80g (2¾oz/generous ⅓ cup) caster (superfine) sugar
3 eggs

Add the milk, cream and condensed milk to a saucepan with all the spices and salt. Gently heat until steaming – don't let it come to the boil. Remove from the heat, cover and let it infuse for at least an hour, but the longer the better.

Before you make your caramel, have a 900-g (2-lb) loaf pan ready nearby. Add the sugar to a small saucepan and heat gently until it starts to melt. Swirl the pan around once in a while to make sure it's melting evenly. Once the sugar melts and turns a deep amber colour, quickly but carefully pour the caramel into the loaf pan. Tilt the pan around so the caramel covers the base, but be careful as it will be very hot. Set aside to cool completely and harden.

Preheat the oven to 160°C (140°C fan/325°F/gas mark 3).

In a bowl, gently whisk your eggs to break them up. Try not to incorporate too much air into them. Strain the infused milk into the egg mixture and mix to combine. Pour the mixture straight on the hardened caramel, cover with some plastic wrap and place the loaf pan in a larger roasting dish or pan.

Fill the roasting dish with hot but not boiling water until it reaches halfway up the sides of the loaf pan. Place it in the oven and bake for 40–50 minutes until the edges of the flan are set but the middle still has a bit of a wobble.

Remove from the oven and take the pan out of the water bath. Let it cool completely for a couple of hours before covering and chilling in the fridge overnight.

When you're ready to serve, run around the edges of the flan with a palette knife. Place your serving platter on top of the pan and quickly but firmly flip the flan over. The caramel will have softened and the flan should slide out fairly easily, but you may have to give it a little shake and tap to help it along.

Spoon any caramel that's left in the pan over the flan and slice to serve.

gingerbread roulade

When it comes to Christmas, one dessert just won't do. I want it all, something hot and rich, something fruity and something spiced and creamy. Like this. Typically, I tend to stay away from biscuit spreads – they're just not my vibe – but here it works so well in tying the gingerbread flavours together alongside the stem ginger and ground spices. Meringue roulades are always impressive and so satisfying when you cut that first slice and see everything swirled together.

Serves 8–10

70g (2½oz/generous ⅓ cup) dark brown sugar
200g (7oz/1 cup) caster (superfine) sugar
¼ tsp ground cloves
2 tsp ground ginger
½ tsp ground cinnamon
200g (7oz) egg whites (from 5 large eggs)
1½ tsp cornflour (cornstarch)
1 tsp white wine vinegar

For the filling

350ml (12fl oz/1½ cups) double (heavy) cream
1 tsp ground ginger
1 Tbsp stem ginger syrup (from the jar of stem ginger)
1 tsp vanilla bean paste
80g (2¾oz) Biscoff biscuit spread
60g (2¼oz) stem ginger, finely chopped

Preheat the oven to 200°C (180°C fan/ 400°F/gas mark 6). Line a baking tray at least 1cm (½in) deep with baking paper

Mix the sugars in a bowl with the spices.

Add the egg whites to a clean, grease-free bowl. Whip on low speed until frothy. Increase the speed to medium-high and whip until you have soft peaks. With the mixer or electric whisk still running, start adding the spiced sugar mixture a tablespoon at a time, waiting about 20 seconds before adding more.

Once you've added all the sugar, the meringue should be thick and glossy, with stiff peaks. Add in the cornflour and whip again briefly until combined. Add in the vinegar and whip to combine.

Spoon the meringue onto the lined tray and use a spatula to spread it out evenly.

Bake for 22–25 minutes until the meringue is puffed up and the surface feels dry to the touch.

Turn the oven off and let it cool inside for 30 minutes. Remove from the oven to let it cool completely.

While it cools, make the filling. Add the cream, ground ginger, stem ginger syrup and vanilla to a bowl and whip until it thickens just a little, before you get to soft peaks. Stir in the biscuit spread and whip until it thickens to a spoonable consistency. Stir in the chopped stem ginger and set aside.

When the meringue is completely cool, Place a sheet of baking paper on the counter and quickly but confidently flip the roulade upside down. Peel off the baking paper that is now on the top. Spoon the filling evenly across the surface and, with a long side facing you, roll up the meringue, using the baking paper underneath to help you.

Place the roulade on a serving platter or board and chill in the fridge until ready to serve.

MAKE AHEAD

Best made on the day.

baked maple cheesecake with roasted pumpkin seeds

MAKE AHEAD

Make 1–2 days in advance and store in an airtight container in the fridge.

I think I've covered all my bases with cheesecakes in this chapter to give you something that fits just about every occasion. This is more of a classic baked cheesecake that is almost guaranteed to go down well at any event. It leans more on the autumnal side with lots of dark maple syrup and crunchy pumpkin seeds bringing the earthy, cosy vibes. When it comes to cheesecake, texture is important. I like mine a little dense but still silky, and I've found the best way to achieve this is by baking in a water bath. I know it feels like a faffy, unnecessary step, but trust me, it's a reliable method for a gentle bake that means you're less likely to overcook the batter and end up with something grainy and cloying.

Serves 12–16

For the base

150g (5½oz) digestive biscuits (graham crackers)
30g (1oz/2½ Tbsp) light brown sugar
70g (2½oz/scant ⅓ cup) unsalted butter, melted

For the filling

600g (1lb 5oz/2⅔ cups) cream cheese, at room temperature
70g (2½oz/generous ⅓ cup) caster (superfine) sugar
125ml (4¼fl oz/generous ½ cup) maple syrup, plus extra to serve
1 tsp vanilla bean paste
3 eggs
170g (6oz/⅔ cup) sour cream
2 tsp plain (all-purpose) flour
¼ tsp fine sea salt

Preheat the oven to 190°C (170°C fan/375°F/gas mark 5). Line the base of a 20-cm (8-in) round loose-bottomed or springform cake pan.

Add the biscuits and brown sugar to a food processor and blitz until fine. Alternatively, add them to a food bag, seal, and bash with a rolling pin. Pour the mixture into a bowl and mix in the melted butter, stirring to coat evenly.

Press the crumbs firmly and evenly into the pan and bake for 10 minutes. Remove from the oven and set aside to cool. Turn the oven temperature down to 160°C (140°C fan/325°F/gas mark 3).

Wrap the outside of the cake pan tightly with a sheet of plastic wrap and then 2 layers of foil. Place the wrapped pan in a larger roasting tray or baking dish and set aside.

To make the filling, add the cream cheese, caster sugar, maple syrup and vanilla to a large bowl and mix until smooth. Mix in the eggs one at a time, followed by the sour cream.

Stir in the flour and salt, mixing well to get rid of any lumps and then pour the batter into the prepared cake pan. Add hot, but not boiling, water to the roasting tray or dish that the cheesecake is sitting in until it reaches about halfway up the sides of the cake pan.

continued overleaf

baked maple cheesecake with roasted pumpkin seeds continued

For the pumpkin seeds

30g (1oz/¼ cup) pumpkin seeds
2 Tbsp maple syrup
pinch of flaky sea salt
pinch of ground cinnamon

To serve

200ml (7fl oz/scant 1 cup) double (heavy) cream, lightly whipped

Bake for 45–50 minutes until the edges of the cheesecake are set but the middle still has a jiggle. Turn off the oven and let the cheesecake cool inside for 30 minutes. Remove from the oven and let it cool completely to room temperature before chilling in the fridge for a couple of hours.

To make the roasted pumpkin seeds, preheat the oven to 180°C (160°C fan/ 350°F/gas mark 4). Line a baking tray with baking paper and add the pumpkin seeds. Pour the maple syrup on top as well as the salt and cinnamon.

Give everything a good stir to coat and bake for 10–12 minutes. Let them cool completely before breaking up into smaller pieces.

When you're ready to serve, top the cheesecake with the whipped cream, pumpkin seeds and more maple syrup if you like.

mango millefeuille pudding

You could describe this as a shortcut millefeuille. A version with all the same elements but infinitely easier to bring along as it's all made in one dish. And also easier to eat. A win-win! I live for a good scoopable dessert; it allows you to be more generous with portions and means you can bring it to the table and let everyone serve themselves. I always use shop-bought puff pastry for this – if you can get an all-butter one, even better.

Serves 6

1 x 320g (11¼oz) sheet of ready-rolled, all-butter puff pastry
2 Tbsp icing (confectioners') sugar, plus extra to serve

For the filling
6 egg yolks
100g (3½oz/½ cup) caster (superfine) sugar
35g (1¼oz/3½ Tbsp) cornflour (cornstarch)
350ml (12fl oz/1½ cups) milk
150g (5½oz) mango purée (canned is great!)
1 ripe mango
grated zest of 1 lime, plus extra to finish
1 Tbsp finely chopped stem ginger (in syrup)
150ml (5fl oz/scant ⅔ cup) double (heavy) cream
½ tsp vanilla bean paste

Preheat the oven to 210°C (190°C fan/410°F/gas mark 6).

Unroll the puff pastry and place it on a sheet of baking paper. Dust the surface generously with the icing sugar, lightly pressing it into the pastry. Flip it over and repeat. Cover with another sheet of baking paper and then put a baking tray that's big enough to cover the pastry on top (this helps weigh it down). Bake for 20–25 minutes until the pastry is cooked through and a deep brown colour. Let it cool completely and set it aside for later.

Add the egg yolks and sugar to a bowl and whisk until smooth. Whisk in the cornflour until you have no lumps.

Heat the milk in a saucepan until steaming but not boiling. Pour a third of the milk onto the eggs and whisk to combine. Continue adding the milk a little at a time, while whisking. Once you've added all the milk, pour everything back into the saucepan and mix in the mango purée. Heat gently while stirring constantly and the custard will start to thicken after 2–3 minutes. Once it starts bubbling, keep cooking it for another 30 seconds before removing from the heat.

Pour it through a sieve (strainer) into a clean, shallow bowl and cover with some plastic wrap that touches the surface of the custard. Let it cool to room temperature before chilling in the fridge for 3–4 hours or until cold.

continued overleaf

MAKE AHEAD

Make and assemble up to 1 day ahead.

mango millefeuille pudding continued

When you're ready to assemble, peel the mango and chop into roughly 2-cm (¾-in) cubes. Toss it in a bowl with the lime zest and ginger.

Whisk the custard by hand to remove any lumps. In a separate bowl, whip the cream and vanilla until just before you get soft peaks. Be careful not to overwhip it.

Fold the cream into the mango custard until combined and set aside.

Slice up the puff pastry with a sharp knife into rough squares that will fit into your chosen serving dish.

Add a layer of the mango custard to your dish followed by a layer of puff pastry squares. Add another layer of custard followed by half of the chopped mango. Add some more pastry on top and then the rest of the custard. Finish it off with any remaining pastry and the rest of the mango. Chill in the fridge and dust with icing (confectioners') sugar and lime zest before serving.

something nutty

Going through this chapter, I'm grateful that I can eat and enjoy nuts without reacting. Nuts are so versatile, with each one bringing its own personality and texture. Hazelnuts and pistachios somehow feel fancy without even trying, whereas walnuts and almonds instantly give me a more cosy, homely feel. Whichever nut you go for in this chapter, you're guaranteed a good time.

peanut butter & blackberry tart

MAKE AHEAD

Make up to 1 day ahead and store in an airtight container at room temperature.

Frangipane tarts will always be a staple in my dessert rotation. They are endlessly customizable and a good option for both casual and fancy settings. Here, I've gone for the classic sweet and salty combination that just always works. Peanut butter is a powerhouse of an ingredient on its own but when paired with a sweet jam, it brings a playfulness and nostalgia that I can't get enough of.

Serves 8–12

2½ Tbsp blackberry or blackcurrant jam (jelly)
100g (3½oz) fresh blackberries
40g (1½oz/⅓ cup) roasted salted peanuts, roughly chopped

For the pastry

180g (6¼oz/1⅓ cups) plain (all-purpose) flour, plus extra for dusting
50g (1¾oz/5¾ Tbsp) icing (confectioners') sugar
¼ tsp fine sea salt
100g (3½oz/scant ½ cup) cold unsalted butter, diced
1 egg yolk
1 Tbsp cold water

For the peanut frangipane

80g (2¾oz/⅓ cup) unsalted butter, softened
100g (3½oz/½ cup) caster (superfine) sugar
35g (1¼oz/generous 2 Tbsp) crunchy peanut butter
1 tsp vanilla bean paste
1 egg
15g (½oz/1½ Tbsp) plain (all-purpose) flour
100g (3½oz/1 cup) ground almonds

To make the pastry, add the flour, icing sugar, salt and butter to a food processor or large bowl. Pulse the mixture to get fine breadcrumbs or rub the butter into the flour with your fingertips until fine. Add the egg yolk and water and pulse again (if making by hand, make a well in the dry ingredients, add the egg yolk and water and stir with a table knife) until the dough starts to clump together.

Turn the dough out onto a lightly floured surface and use your hands to gently bring it together. Pat it into a thick disc, wrap in plastic wrap and chill in the fridge for 2 hours or until firm.

Roll out the pastry onto a lightly floured surface and use it to line a 23-cm (9-in) tart pan, leaving a bit of overhang around the edges. Prick the base with a fork and chill the tart in the freezer for 15 minutes.

Preheat the oven to 190°C (170°C fan/ 375°F/gas mark 5).

Line the tart pan with baking paper or foil Fill with baking beans or uncooked rice and bake for 17 minutes, until the edges start to brown. Remove the baking beans and paper and return to the oven for 7 minutes. Remove from the oven and set aside to cool while you make the filling.

For the frangipane, add the butter and sugar to a bowl and cream together until creamy. Mix in the peanut butter and vanilla. Beat in the egg, followed by the flour and ground almonds.

Spoon the jam into the tart case, spreading it out evenly. Top with the frangipane and add the berries on top. Sprinkle with the peanuts and bake for 30–35 minutes until golden. Let it cool completely before serving.

baci di dama

These cute little Italian biscuits are a top choice for an after-dinner coffee accompaniment. With just enough sweetness to round off a meal, they also double up as the perfect edible gift to send away with guests. I've added a little chopped candied peel in these, which isn't at all traditional but I love the citrusy bitterness it brings.

Makes 20–23

80g (2¾oz/⅔ cup) blanched hazelnuts
80g (2¾oz/scant ⅔ cup) plain (all-purpose) flour
80g (2¾oz/generous ⅓ cup) caster (superfine) sugar
80g (2¾oz/⅓ cup) salted butter, softened
1 Tbsp finely chopped candied peel
100g (3½oz) dark chocolate

Preheat the oven to 170°C (150°C fan/ 325°F/gas mark 3).

Add the hazelnuts to a baking tray and toast in the oven for 12–15 minutes or until nicely browned and fragrant.

Let them cool completely before adding to a food processor along with the flour and sugar. Pulse until the nuts are finely ground. Add the butter and pulse again until the butter is well incorporated. Add the candied peel and give it a quick pulse.

Tip the mixture out onto your work surface and use your hands to gently knead for a few seconds to bring it together. Place the dough on a small baking tray lined with baking paper and flatten it out about 2.5cm (½in) thick. Cover with plastic wrap and chill for 1–2 hours until firm.

Preheat the oven to 170°C (150°C fan/ 325°F/gas mark 3).

Once chilled, use a sharp knife to slice the dough into 40–46 portions and roll each one into a ball. Place them on 2 lined baking trays, leaving about 1cm (½in) between them.

Bake for 15–17 minutes or until lightly browned. Let them cool completely.

Melt the chocolate in the microwave or in a bowl set over a pan of simmering water, making sure the base of the bowl isn't touching the water. Let the filling cool until it starts to thicken a little. If it's too runny, it will spill out of the biscuits.

Spoon or pipe about a ¼ teaspoon on the base of half of your biscuits. Sandwich with another biscuit, being careful not to squish them too much. Let them set completely before serving or boxing up.

MAKE AHEAD

Make the biscuits, unfilled, up to 3 days in advance and store in an airtight container. Add the chocolate up to 1 day before serving.

hazelnut & marmalade meringue cake

MAKE AHEAD

Both the meringue and custard can be made up to 2 days before. Assemble and chill on the day you want to serve.

I could very easily sit and eat the meringue layers in this cake. They make such a good little snack – sweet and crisp with slightly chewy edges. But to make this a proper dessert, I've filled it with a light pastry cream folded in with some marmalade for a subtle lift of citrus. As with anything in this book, you can make and eat any of the recipes whenever you fancy but this does feel more like an 'occasion' cake. Something I'd make for a special candlelit evening or for the festive season. Either way, make it more manageable by baking the meringues and preparing the custard the day before and then just assemble a few hours ahead.

Serves 12

For the meringue

100g (3½oz/¾ cup) blanched hazelnuts
180g (6¼oz/scant 1 cup) caster (superfine) sugar
3 egg whites (about 135g/4¾oz)
10g (1 Tbsp) cornflour (cornstarch)

For the filling

1 egg, plus 3 egg yolks
80g (2¾oz/generous ⅓ cup) caster (superfine) sugar
20g (¾oz/2 Tbsp) cornflour (cornstarch)
200ml (7fl oz/scant 1 cup) milk
300ml (10½fl oz/generous 1¼ cups) double (heavy) cream
¼ tsp fine sea salt
½ tsp vanilla bean paste
10g (¾ Tbsp) unsalted butter, softened
70g (2½oz) marmalade, plus extra for dolloping

To finish

icing (confectioners') sugar

Preheat the oven to 180°C (160°C fan/ 350°F/gas mark 4).

Add the hazelnuts to a baking tray and toast for 12–15 minutes until lightly browned and fragrant. Set aside to cool and then blitz in a food processor with 30g (1oz/2½ Tbsp) of the sugar until fine.

Turn the oven down to 160°C (140°C fan/ 325°F/gas mark 3) and line 2 baking trays with baking paper. Draw a 20-cm (8-in) circle template on each piece of paper using a plate or cake pan to guide you. Turn the paper upside down so the pencil outlines are facing downwards.

Add the egg whites to the bowl of a stand mixer and whisk on low speed for 30 seconds before increasing the speed to medium-high. Once the egg whites are white with soft peaks, add in the remaining sugar a tablespoon at a time, leaving about 20 seconds between each addition. Once all the sugar has gone in, the egg whites should be thick and glossy with stiff peaks.

Add the cornflour and whisk for a few more seconds to combine. Tip the ground hazelnuts on top and use a spatula to gently fold them into the meringue.

Spoon the mixture into a large piping (pastry) bag, snip off the end and, starting from the centre of your templates and working your way outwards, pipe a spiral onto each tray.

Bake for 40–45 minutes until the meringues look dry to the touch. Turn off the oven and let them cool completely inside to help them dry out. This will take about 50–60 minutes. Once cool, set aside or store in an airtight container until ready to use.

To make the filling, add the whole egg and yolks to a bowl and mix to combine. Mix in the sugar and cornflour to get a smooth consistency. Add the milk, 200ml (7fl oz/scant 1 cup) of the cream, the salt and vanilla to a small saucepan. Heat gently until steaming and then pour about a quarter onto the eggs, whisking at the same time. Continue pouring in the hot milk while whisking, and then pour everything back into the saucepan.

Gently heat while stirring continuously until the custard thickens and starts bubbling. Remove from the heat and stir in the butter until it melts. Stir in the marmalade and pour the custard into a clean, shallow bowl. Cover with plastic wrap that touches the surface and let it cool to room temperature before chilling in the fridge for 3–4 hours or until well chilled.

When ready to assemble, lightly whip the remaining 100ml (3½fl oz/scant ½ cup) cream. Whisk the custard well to loosen and remove any lumps. Carefully fold the whipped cream into the custard.

Place one of the meringues on your serving plate or cake board. Spoon or pipe the custard on top and add small dollops of extra marmalade, top with the other meringue. Chill in the fridge until you're ready to serve, dusting with icing sugar right before serving.

pistachio & fresh mint panna cotta

MAKE AHEAD

Make the panna cotta up to 2 days ahead. Turn them out of the moulds right before serving.

Panna cotta is a deceptively simple dessert. You can infuse pretty much any flavour you fancy for a light and delicate pudding that melts in the mouth. Here, the pistachio paste brings a creamy nuttiness and the fresh mint brightens it all up with a herbal undertone. Most pistachio pastes come sweetened but if you're using a pistachio butter, you'll need to up the sugar by 20–30g (¾–1oz).

Serves 4

- neutral oil (such as sunflower or vegetable), for greasing
- 3 gelatine leaves (platinum grade)
- 350ml (12fl oz/1½ cups) double (heavy) cream
- 250ml (9fl oz/generous 1 cup) milk
- 30g (1oz/2½ Tbsp) caster (superfine) sugar
- 5g (¼oz) fresh mint leaves
- 60g (2¼oz) pistachio paste
- 20g (¾oz/generous ¼ cup) pistachios, roughly chopped

Very lightly grease 4 panna cotta moulds with a little oil (if you're using ramekins or won't be turning the panna cotta out, then skip this step).

Add the gelatine to a small bowl of cold water and let it soak for 5 minutes.

Add the cream, milk and sugar to a small pan and heat gently until steaming and the sugar has dissolved. Remove from the heat and add in the mint leaves. Cover and let it infuse for 30–60 minutes.

Strain the milk into a jug (pitcher) and discard the mint leaves. Add the pistachio paste to the pan and pour in the cream and milk mixture a little at a time while stirring, to dissolve the pistachio paste. Once it has all been added, gently reheat to warm the mixture and then take off the heat.

Stir in the soaked gelatine leaves, squeezing them before adding to get rid of any excess water.

Pour the mixture into your moulds or ramekins. Let them cool to room temperature before chilling in the fridge for 6 hours or overnight, until set.

When you're ready to serve, dip the moulds quickly into a bowl of hot (but not boiling) water, put a plate on top and flip to remove. The hot water should have loosened them enough to fall out easily but if they don't slide out, give them a little shake or re-dip in the hot water.

Top with the chopped pistachios before serving. These also go well with the tuiles on page 185.

olive oil & toasted almond cake with burnt honey cream

Everyone should have a couple of one-bowl cake recipes up their sleeve. And this one is particularly good. It's the sort of cake that works for nearly all occasions where you might be asked to bring a dessert. It's simple enough to make on the same day you need it but different enough that it feels special yet still familiar. The burnt honey cream is a little addictive; I'll often make more than I need just to pour on anything else, so don't skip it!

Serves 8–10

60g (2¼oz/scant ½ cup) whole almonds, skin on
135g (4¾oz/generous ½ cup) olive oil, plus extra for greasing
170g (6oz/generous ¾ cup) caster (superfine) sugar
2 large eggs
1 tsp vanilla bean paste
50ml (2fl oz/3½ Tbsp) milk
160g (5¾oz/scant 1¼ cups) plain (all-purpose) flour
1½ tsp baking powder
pinch of fine sea salt
20g (¾oz/¼ cup) flaked (slivered) almonds

For the burnt honey cream
150g (5½oz/½ cup) honey
250ml (9fl oz/generous 1 cup) whipping (heavy) cream
pinch of fine sea salt

Preheat the oven to 180°C (160°C fan/350°F/gas mark 4). Grease a 20-cm (8-in) round cake pan and line with baking paper.

Add the whole almonds to a baking tray and roast in the oven for 15–18 minutes until well browned and toasty. Let them cool completely before blitzing in a food processor until fine.

Add the olive oil, sugar, eggs and vanilla to a bowl and give it a good whisk to combine. Stir in the milk.

Add the flour, ground almonds, baking powder and salt and mix until smooth. Pour the batter into the prepared cake pan and top with the flaked almonds

Bake for 30–35 minutes until lightly browned and a skewer inserted into the centre comes out clean. Set aside to cool completely.

Add the honey to a small saucepan and let it come to the boil, swirling the pan often so it heats evenly. Once it darkens to a deep amber, remove from the heat and pour in the cream. Be careful as it will splutter and spit. Give it a good stir to combine, add in the salt and pour into a bowl to cool. Chill in the fridge until cold. You can serve this with the cake as a pouring cream or whip it up to get soft peaks.

MAKE AHEAD

Make the cake up to 2 days in advance.

walnut cardamom coffee cake

MAKE AHEAD

The cake can be made up to 2 days in advance. Make and ice the cake on the day you want to serve.

There's a reason coffee and walnut cake is a British classic that appears to have stood the test of time. If you're bringing something to a coffee morning, bake sale or afternoon catch up, then this is a solid option that even people who don't like coffee will find difficult not to have a slice or two of. I've spiked this version with a bit of cardamom because, yes, it's my favourite spice, but also because it brings some brightness and freshness that I think works really well.

Serves 8–10

100g (3½oz/1 cup) walnuts
8 green cardamom pods
2 eggs
200g (7oz/1 cup) light brown sugar
170ml (5½fl oz/scant ¾ cup) neutral oil (such as sunflower or vegetable)
80ml (2½fl oz/⅓ cup) brewed coffee
200g (7oz/1½ cups) plain (all-purpose) flour
1½ tsp baking powder
½ tsp bicarbonate of soda (baking soda)
¼ tsp fine sea salt
60g (2¼oz/¼ cup) plain yoghurt

For the topping

50g (1¾oz/3½ Tbsp) unsalted butter, softened
140g (5oz/1 cup) icing (confectioners') sugar
280g (10oz/1¼ cups) cream cheese
1 tsp espresso powder

Preheat the oven to 180°C (160°C fan/350°F/gas mark 4). Grease a 20-cm (8-in) round cake pan and line with baking paper.

Add the walnuts to a baking tray and roast for 7–8 minutes until toasty. Let them cool and set a few aside to top the cake. Add the rest to a food processor and blitz until you have a coarse texture – you don't want a fine powder here.

Crack open the cardamom pods and remove the seeds. Add them to a pestle and mortar and grind up to as fine as you can. Set aside.

Add the eggs, sugar and oil to a bowl and whisk briefly to combine. Stir in the coffee. Add the flour, ground cardamom and walnuts, baking powder, bicarbonate of soda and salt and fold gently to combine. Stir in the yoghurt and pour the batter into the prepared cake pan.

Bake for 35–40 minutes until deeply golden and a skewer inserted into the centre comes out clean. Let it cool completely.

To make the topping, add the butter and icing sugar to a bowl and cream together until thick and smooth. Beat in the cream cheese and espresso powder and mix until smooth.

Spoon it all on top of the cake and use the back of a spoon to smooth it out. Top with the leftover walnuts before serving.

roasted plantains & peanuts with tamarind

MAKE AHEAD

Best made on the day of serving.

Such is the greatness and versatility of plantains you can have them for breakfast, lunch, dinner and even dessert. Pairing them with peanuts is a classic combination and both are roasted well for maximum flavour. If you're bringing something to a BBQ, these are a great option. Add them to the grill once the coals are cooling down and serve hot, with puddles of condensed milk.

Serves 8–10

100g (3½oz/scant 1 cup) salted peanuts, roughly chopped
2½ Tbsp tamarind paste
1½ tsp ground cinnamon
1½ Tbsp brown sugar
4 ripe plantains

To serve
condensed milk
flaky sea salt

Preheat the oven to 200°C (180°C fan/400°F/gas mark 6).

Add the peanuts to a lined baking tray and roast for 15–18 minutes until well browned. Set aside to cool.

Mix the tamarind, cinnamon and sugar together in a bowl.

Peel the plantains and place them on a BBQ or in an oven preheated to 220°C (200°C fan/425°F/gas mark 7). Cook for 15–25 minutes, turning frequently until the plantain is softened and charred but still holding its shape. Brush with some of the tamarind mixture and roast for another 5 minutes, until sticky.

Move the plantains to a board or platter and cut into 1-cm (½-in) thick slices. Top with the peanuts, a drizzle of condensed milk and some flaky sea salt. Serve hot.

rum & raisin pecan loaf

Rum and raisin as a pairing has a bit of an old-school feel to it but it's a faithful classic. If you're incredibly organized (I am not) you can soak the raisins up to two days in advance for maximum booziness, but more often than not I'll just give them at least an hour and I've not had any complaints. My favourite way to serve this is warmed with plenty of crème anglaise (page 176), but for those of you who like things over-the-top, then a scoop of rum and raisin ice cream would be just as fun.

Serves 8

100ml (3½fl oz/scant ½ cup) dark rum
120g (4¼oz/scant 1 cup) raisins
175g (6oz/¾ cup) unsalted butter, softened, plus extra for greasing
200g (7oz/1 cup) light muscovado sugar
grated zest of 1 orange
30g (1oz/1½ Tbsp) treacle
2 eggs
225g (8oz/1¾ cups) plain (all-purpose) flour
1 tsp ground cinnamon
¼ tsp ground cloves
2 tsp baking powder
½ tsp bicarbonate of soda (baking soda)
pinch of fine sea salt
60g (2¼oz/¼ cup) ricotta
60g (2¼oz/½ cup) pecans, roughly chopped

For the syrup

50g (1¾oz/¼ cup) light muscovado sugar
50ml (2fl oz/3½ Tbsp) water

Add the rum to a small pan and heat gently until warmed through – don't let it come to the boil. Remove from the heat and add in the raisins. Cover and set aside and let the raisins soak for a couple of hours, or overnight.

Preheat the oven to 180°C (160°C fan/350°F/gas mark 4). Grease a 900-g (2-lb) loaf pan and line with baking paper.

Add the butter, sugar and orange zest to a bowl and cream together with an electric whisk for 3–4 minutes until pale and creamy. Add in the treacle and mix to combine, then add the eggs one at a time, beating well after each addition.

In a separate bowl, sift together the flour, cinnamon, cloves, baking powder, bicarbonate of soda and salt. Stir this into the butter mixture until thick and smooth, and then mix in the ricotta.

Drain the raisins from the rum, keeping the rum for later. Add the raisins and pecans to the batter, stirring in gently to evenly disperse. Spoon the batter into the lined pan, smooth the top and bake for 50–55 minutes until a skewer inserted into the centre comes out clean.

While the cake bakes, add the sugar and water for the syrup to a small pan and bring to the boil. Let it simmer for a few minutes or until the sugar has dissolved and it looks syrupy. Remove from the heat and pour in the leftover rum.

Prick the surface of the cake with a skewer or toothpick and pour the syrup over the warm cake. Leave to cool completely before serving with crème anglaise or cream.

MAKE AHEAD

Make the loaf up to 2 days ahead and keep it well wrapped.

hazelnut puff tart

MAKE AHEAD

The tart can be made up to 1 day ahead and stored in the fridge.

This is essentially a short-cut galette des rois, which is a traditional French pastry usually eaten throughout January to celebrate Epiphany. It's usually made with almonds, but I love mine with hazelnuts and a hint of coffee. It's a beautiful tart with puffy layers of flaky pastry and a nutty, squidgy middle. You can serve this at room temperature but I think it's best when warmed through and served with a splash of cold cream.

Serves 8–10

100g (3½oz/¾ cup) blanched hazelnuts
80g (2¾oz/⅓ cup) unsalted butter, softened
100g (3½oz/½ cup) caster (superfine) sugar
1 tsp espresso powder
1 tsp vanilla bean paste
1 egg, plus 1 extra egg, beaten, for glazing
¼ tsp fine sea salt
2 x 320g (11¼oz) sheets of ready-rolled, all-butter puff pastry

Preheat the oven to 190°C (170°C fan/375°F/gas mark 5). Line a large baking tray with baking paper.

Add the hazelnuts to the tray and toast in the oven for 12–15 minutes or until lightly browned and fragrant. Let them cool completely before blitzing in a food processor until fine. Set the lined tray aside until you need it again.

Add the butter, sugar, espresso powder and vanilla to a bowl and use an electric whisk to beat until pale and fluffy. Add the egg and mix again to combine. Stir in the ground hazelnuts and salt. Spoon the mixture into a large piping (pastry) bag and place it in the fridge for 20 minutes.

Unroll one sheet of puff pastry and cut out a 20-cm (8-in) circle. (You can use an upturned plate to help you.) Place it straight on the lined baking tray. Starting from the centre, start piping the frangipane in a spiral, leaving about 2cm (¾in) clear around the edges. Brush the exposed edges with some egg wash.

Unroll the second sheet of pastry and cut out another circle about 22cm (8½in) wide. Place this on top of the frangipane and press down the edges firmly to seal. Crimp the edges with a knife (make evenly spaced indents all around the edges) and then chill in the fridge for 30 minutes.

Preheat the oven to 190°C (170°C fan/375°F/gas mark 5). Brush the surface of the tart with beaten egg and use a skewer to make a little hole in the middle to allow steam to escape. Use a sharp knife to score a pattern on the surface and bake for 35–40 minutes until well risen and deeply browned. Let it cool completely before serving with cold cream.

marzipan yoghurt cakes

I know there'll be plenty of you who see the word marzipan and quickly turn the page – I used to be one of those people, so I get it. But over the years I've been converted and have had fun playing around with it in different desserts. These cakes may just change your mind too. If you like that artificial almond essence flavour you get in things like Bakewell tarts, then you'll love this. They stay incredibly soft for days and the texture is almost pudding like. You could simply dust these with a little icing sugar to serve but I love them with a good dollop of lightly sweetened yoghurt on top, and a seasonal jam or compote.

Makes 5

90g (3¼oz/⅓ cup plus 1 Tbsp) unsalted butter, softened, plus extra for greasing
125g (4½oz/1¼ cups) ground almonds, plus extra for dusting
125g (4½oz) marzipan
75g (2½oz/6 Tbsp) caster (superfine) sugar
2 eggs
1 tsp baking powder
¼ tsp fine sea salt
60g (2¼oz/¼ cup) Greek yoghurt

To serve
200g (7oz/scant 1 cup) Greek yoghurt
½ Tbsp icing (confectioners') sugar
jam (jelly) or compote

Preheat the oven to 180°C (160°C fan/350°F/gas mark 4). Grease 5 holes of a large 6-hole muffin tray and place a circle of baking paper in the base of each. Dust the edges generously with ground almonds.

Add the butter and marzipan to a food processor and blitz until combined. Add in the sugar and eggs and blitz again until smooth, making sure to scrape down the sides frequently.

Tip in the almonds, baking powder and salt and pulse to combine. Spoon in the yoghurt and give it one last blitz. Spoon the batter evenly into the holes and bake for 30–35 minutes until risen and browned.

Let them cool in the tray for 5 minutes before running a spatula around the edges to loosen. Tip them out onto a wire rack, upside down, to cool completely.

To serve, mix the yoghurt and icing sugar together until smooth. Spoon a little on top of each cake and top with jam or compote before serving.

MAKE AHEAD

The cakes can be made 2 days in advance, but make the yoghurt topping on the day you are serving.

apple, walnut & pistachio filo bake

MAKE AHEAD

The pre-baked pudding can stay well wrapped in the fridge overnight. Once baked, it's best eaten on the day it's made.

This is a good autumnal pudding. If desserts were months, this would definitely be October, or maybe November. Warming and cosy for those colder, darker evenings but still relatively light, it hasn't quite hit the levels of stodge and heartiness that would be required for winter. It's a bit of a play on a baklava and a strudel, incorporating baked apples, chopped nuts, spice and buttered sheets of filo. Serve this straight from the oven when the filo is still crisp and the apples still plump and warm.

Serves 6

40g (1½oz/scant ½ cup) walnuts
60g (2¼oz/½ cup) pistachios, plus extra chopped to finish
50g (1¾oz/3½ Tbsp) salted butter or ghee, melted, plus extra for greasing
1 Tbsp demerara (turbinado) sugar
4 eating apples (I use Braeburn or Cox)
75g (2½oz/6 Tbsp) light brown sugar
1 tsp ground cinnamon
½ tsp ground ginger
¼ tsp freshly grated nutmeg
grated zest and juice of ½ orange
2 tsp tamarind paste
3 sheets of filo (phyllo) pastry

Add all the walnuts and pistachios to a food processor and pulse until you have a coarse mixture. You don't want them too fine, so a few chunks are okay.

Preheat the oven to 200°C (180°C fan/400°F/gas mark 6). Prepare a baking dish, about 21 x 27cm (8¼ x 10½in), by buttering the base and covering with the demerara sugar.

Peel and core the apples and slice each into 8. Add them to a bowl with the light brown sugar, spices, orange zest and juice and the tamarind. Give it a good mix to coat and set aside for 15 minutes.

Place one sheet of filo on a tray. Brush the surface generously with melted butter and place the next layer of filo on top. Brush with more butter and place the last layer on top of that, brushing with more butter to finish.

Cut the filo into 8 squares and sprinkle some of the nut mixture on each. Place 4 pieces of apple in each square and fold up the filo, leaving the apple exposed – like a taco. Reserve the juices left in the bowl. Place the filo pieces sitting upright in the dish and repeat with the rest of the squares, making sure they are all snug.

Bake for 45–50 minutes until the filo looks well browned

Meanwhile, add the leftover juices from the apple to a small pan and heat gently until it looks syrupy.

Pour the syrup over the filo and put it back in the oven for another 2 minutes. Remove from the oven and let it cool for 15 minutes before topping with the extra chopped pistachios and serving warm with cream or ice cream.

pistachio gâteau Basque

MAKE AHEAD

Make the gâteau up to 1 day ahead. Or break the process into chunks and make the custard up to 3 days in advance and the dough the day before.

A gâteau Basque has quite a unique texture; it's a bit of a cross between a tart and a cake and usually sandwiched together with either pastry cream or jam. And in this version, I've gone for both.

If you're someone who likes a bit of a project bake every now and again, then this is for you. It's not that it's a super-technical bake, it just takes a bit of time and patience as it needs lots of chilling between steps. Definitely not one for a last-minute dessert option, so make this for people you really, really like.

Serves 8–10

2 Tbsp cherry jam (jelly)
1 egg, beaten

For the pastry
85g (3oz/scant ¾ cup) pistachios
130g (4¾oz/½ cup plus 1 Tbsp) salted butter, softened, plus extra for greasing
100g (3½oz/½ cup) caster (superfine) sugar
1 egg, plus 1 egg yolk
180g (6¼oz/1⅓ cups) plain (all-purpose) flour
1 tsp baking powder
¼ tsp fine sea salt

For the custard
1 egg, plus 2 egg yolks
60g (2¼oz/5 Tbsp) caster (superfine) sugar
80g (2¾oz) pistachio paste
30g (1oz/3 Tbsp) cornflour (cornstarch)
350ml (12fl oz/1½ cups) milk
20g (1½ Tbsp) salted butter

To make the pastry, add the pistachios to a food processor and grind until fine. Set aside.

Add the butter and sugar to a bowl and cream together until smooth. It doesn't need to be fluffy.

Add in the whole egg and mix to combine before adding in the extra yolk. In a separate bowl, mix together the flour, ground pistachios, baking powder and salt. Add this to the butter mixture and mix to get a soft dough.

Spoon it out onto a sheet of plastic wrap and flatten down to about 1cm (½in) thick. Wrap and chill for 3–4 hours, or overnight.

To make the custard, add the whole egg, extra yolks, half of the sugar and the pistachio paste to a bowl and whisk to combine. Add in the cornflour and whisk until smooth.

Add the milk and remaining sugar to a small saucepan and heat gently until steaming – don't let it come to the boil. Slowly pour the hot milk over the eggs, while whisking, and then pour everything back into the saucepan.

Heat gently while stirring continuously until the custard thickens and bubbles. Remove from the heat, pour it through a sieve (strainer) to get rid of any lumps and into a clean bowl. Stir through the butter until melted and cover with some plastic wrap touching the surface. Set aside to cool completely and then chill until needed.

To assemble, grease a 20-cm (8-in) round cake pan or tart pan. Roll out about one-third of the dough between 2 sheets of baking paper to about 5mm (¼in) thick and wide enough to cover the top of the pan. Place this dough, including the baking paper, in the freezer to firm up.

Add the remaining dough to the cake or tart pan and use your fingers to press it in, making sure it's even and pressed into all the edges. Spoon the cherry jam inside and spread it out evenly. Place this in the fridge to firm up for 20 minutes.

Once chilled, spoon the custard over the jam and spread it out evenly. Take out the sheet of dough from the freezer and peel off one sheet of baking paper. Place it dough side down on top of the custard and carefully peel back the remaining paper.

Gently press the edges down to seal and trim off any excess. Place the tart back in the fridge to chill for another 20 minutes.

Preheat the oven to 190°C (170°C fan/ 375°F/gas mark 5).

Brush the top of the gâteau with the beaten egg and use the tip of a sharp knife to score a pattern on top.

Place it on a baking tray and bake for 45–50 minutes until the tart is well browned and risen. Let it cool completely (this could take a couple of hours) before slicing to serve.

pistachio & polenta cake with preserved lemon

A cake that can stay moist for days is a keeper. This cake is a bit of an over-achiever in that respect, with ground pistachios, oil and yoghurt coming together to create a perfectly dense and nutty cake. This is a good all-rounder – something I would take for a casual afternoon or lazy summer evening gathering. But it would also be right at home if you wanted to bring something to impress. Preserved lemons can be a bit divisive but there's just enough here to notice that something different is going on without them being overpowering.

Serves 8–10

100g (3½oz/scant ½ cup) sunflower oil, plus extra for greasing
180g (6¼oz/1½ cups) pistachios, plus extra chopped to decorate
80g (2¾oz/½ cup) polenta (fine cornmeal)
175g (4½oz/scant ⅔ cup) caster (superfine) sugar
¼ tsp bicarbonate of soda (baking soda)
1 tsp baking powder
1 preserved lemon (about 35–40g/ 1¼–1½oz)
2 eggs
80g (2¾oz/⅓ cup) plain yoghurt
grated zest of 1 lemon

For the glaze
180g (6¼oz/1¼ cups) icing (confectioners') sugar
juice of 1 lemon

Preheat the oven to 180°C (160°C fan/ 350°F/gas mark 4). Grease a 20-cm (8-in) round cake pan and line with baking paper.

Add the pistachios to a food processor and blitz until fine. Pour into a bowl along with the polenta, sugar, bicarbonate of soda and baking powder, and set aside.

Cut the preserved lemon in half and remove any seeds. Mash the preserved lemon in a pestle and mortar until you have a paste, or finely chop and smush it on a chopping board.

Add the eggs, oil, yoghurt and lemon zest to a separate bowl. Give it a good whisk and stir in the preserved lemon. Pour this into your dry ingredients and stir to combine.

Pour the batter into the prepared cake pan and bake for 35–40 minutes until browned and a skewer inserted into the centre comes out clean. Let the cake cool completely.

To make the glaze, add the icing sugar to a small bowl, then mix in the lemon juice a little at a time, stopping when the icing is quite thick but still pourable. You may not need all of the lemon juice, but if it gets too thin, just mix in a little more icing sugar.

Spoon the glaze on top of the cake, using the back of a spoon to nudge it towards the edges of the cake. Top with the extra chopped pistachios and let set for 10 minutes before slicing.

MAKE AHEAD

The cake will keep well wrapped for 2 days. Add the glaze on the day of serving.

something on the side

These are all the extra bits, the finishing touches, the supporting acts that help bring some extra crunch, moisture and pizzazz to your desserts. Whether it's a generous pour of homemade custard, a dollop of compote alongside your cake or a hearty sprinkle of caramelized sesame seeds, bring them along in some Tupperware and add to your desserts at the table.

crème anglaise

MAKE AHEAD

Best made on the day if serving hot, but can be made up to 3 days in advance and stored, covered, in the fridge. If reheating, don't use the microwave. Instead place the custard in a bowl set over a pan of simmering water and heat gently, stirring, until warmed through.

A crème anglaise, or runny custard as I sometimes call it, is the mother of all custards. It's smooth, silky and creamy with a beautifully gentle vanilla flavour. Unlike a thicker pastry cream, it's made without cornflour (cornstarch) and goes with just about anything: cakes, poached fruits, hot crumbles, puddings. It's an easy one to whip up quite quickly on the spot, and is one of my most used 'something on the side'. If you're having it hot, it's best eaten as soon as it's made, but I have to say there's an unexplainable joy I get when having it cold from the fridge. Just be careful when cooking and reheating so the eggs don't scramble.

Serves 4–6

4 egg yolks
35g (1¼oz/3 Tbsp) caster (superfine) sugar
250ml (9fl oz/generous 1 cup) milk
200ml (7fl oz/scant 1 cup) double (heavy) cream
1 vanilla pod (bean) or 1 tsp vanilla bean paste

Add the egg yolks and sugar to a bowl and whisk until smooth. Set aside.

Add the milk, cream and vanilla to a small saucepan. (If you're using a vanilla pod, split it open down the middle with a sharp knife and scrape out the seeds. Add both the seeds and pod to the milk.) Heat gently until the milk is hot and steaming, right before it comes to the boil.

Remove from the heat and pour a quarter of the milk onto the eggs, while whisking. Slowly pour in the rest of the milk and then pour everything back into the saucepan.

Heat the mixture very gently for 4–6 minutes over a medium-low heat, stirring with a wooden spoon or spatula and making sure to get into the corners of the pan. Once the custard thickens enough to coat the back of the spoon, remove from the heat and pour it through a sieve (strainer) and into a jug (pitcher) or bowl.

Serve straight away or cover and chill.

chocolate malt custard

MAKE AHEAD

Make up to 2 days ahead and store in the fridge. To reheat, place the custard in a bowl set over a pan of simmering water and heat gently, stirring, until warmed through.

Chocolate custard was a staple on any school-dinner menu in the UK and felt like the best thing since sliced bread when served with a wedge of fluffy chocolate cake. This custard is for when you're in the mood for chocolate on chocolate. The malt extract feels right at home here, bringing deep toasty notes and a subtle earthiness that stops it from being too sweet. Serve this generously with desserts like the chocolate & coconut breadcrumb cake on page 76, the clotted cream chocolate chip cake on page 92, or go completely rogue and try it with the cherry slab pie on page 16. (It works!)

Serves 4–6

4 egg yolks
2 Tbsp caster (superfine) sugar
1 Tbsp unsweetened cocoa powder
1½ tsp cornflour (cornstarch)
500ml (17fl oz/2 cups) milk
1 tsp vanilla bean paste
1 Tbsp malt extract
30g (1oz) dark chocolate, finely chopped

Add the egg yolks, sugar, cocoa powder and cornflour to a bowl and whisk thoroughly until smooth. Set aside.

Add the milk, vanilla and malt extract to a saucepan and heat gently until steaming but not boiling. Remove from the heat and pour a quarter of the hot milk onto the eggs, whisking quickly to combine. Continue adding the milk a little at a time until it's all in.

Pour everything back into the saucepan and heat very gently, stirring frequently with a wooden spoon or spatula and making sure to get into the corners of the pan. After about 5–6 minutes, the custard will begin to thicken. Once it's thick enough to coat the back of the spoon, remove from the heat and stir in the chopped chocolate until melted. Pour it straight into a jug (pitcher) and serve warm.

sour cream crème pât

Crème pâtissière, pastry cream or crème pât, plays such a major role in dessert – particularly in this book. It's so incredibly flexible and is something that, over time, you'll be able to whip up without even thinking. You can flavour crème pât in so many ways, but an easy way to make it a little different without too much effort is to fold in some sour cream at the end. It brightens the whole thing up, bringing a welcome tang that works particularly well alongside fruit- or nut-based desserts. I'll sometimes add a dollop of this instead of whipped cream when I need something with a bit more weight. Try it alongside the saffron & cardamom pear galettes on page 51, or as an alternative topping to the marzipan yoghurt cakes on page 163.

Makes enough for 8–10 servings

3 egg yolks
30g (1oz/2½ Tbsp) golden caster (superfine) sugar
20g (¾oz/2 Tbsp) cornflour (cornstarch)
350ml (12fl oz/1½ cups) milk
½ tsp vanilla bean paste
100g (3½oz/scant ½ cup) sour cream

Add the egg yolks, sugar and cornflour to a bowl and whisk thoroughly until smooth. Set aside.

Add the milk and vanilla to a saucepan and heat gently until steaming but not boiling. Remove from the heat and pour a quarter of the hot milk onto the eggs, whisking quickly to combine. Continue adding the milk a little at a time until it's all in.

Pour everything back into the saucepan and heat gently, stirring frequently with a wooden spoon or spatula and making sure to get into all the corners of the pan. The custard will begin to thicken after 4–5 minutes. Keep stirring, making sure to get into all the corners. Once the custard comes to a boil and starts bubbling, remove from the heat and pour it into a clean bowl. Stir in the sour cream and cover with a sheet of plastic wrap, touching the surface.

Let it cool to room temperature before chilling in the fridge until cold. When ready to use, give it a good whisk to remove any lumps.

MAKE AHEAD

Make up to 3 days ahead and store in the fridge.

coconut whip

MAKE AHEAD

Make the coconut whip up to 2 days ahead and store in the fridge.

Make the hot fudge peanut butter sauce up to 1 week ahead and store in the fridge. Reheat in a small saucepan over a low heat until just warmed through.

This dairy-free whip is not just for the vegans. It's an easy alternative when I want something on the side that's creamy but without the richness of double (heavy) cream. It's deceptively light and airy and brings a subtle coconut flavour that doesn't overpower. Dollop it alongside slices of cake, or use it to fill your vegan pavlovas on page 116 (doubling the quantity).

The key to a good coconut whip is making sure everything is really cold or it just won't hold. Stick the carton of coconut cream in the fridge the night before to make sure it's well chilled. And if I'm making this on a warm day, then I'll even put the bowl in the fridge about an hour before whipping.

Makes enough for 8 servings

250g (9oz/1¼ cups) coconut cream (not to be confused with creamed coconut)
1½ Tbsp icing (confectioners') sugar
½ tsp vanilla extract
2–3 Tbsp dairy-free milk (optional)

Add the chilled coconut cream to a bowl and whip with an electric whisk for 1–2 minutes until creamy and fluffy. Add in the icing sugar and vanilla and whip again until smooth.

If you want a looser consistency, add in some dairy-free milk a tablespoon at a time until you get to what you want. Store in the fridge until ready to use.

hot fudge peanut butter sauce

There's a ridiculous number of recipes in this book that you could serve this with, so I won't bore you by listing them all out, but if you're really strapped for time and need to bring something sweet, then just a jar of this with some good vanilla ice cream and chopped peanuts would be a simple but delicious option.

Makes enough for 10–14 servings

75g (2½oz/6 Tbsp) light brown sugar
60g (2¼oz/3 Tbsp) golden syrup
25g (1oz/¼ cup) unsweetened cocoa powder
275ml (9½fl oz/scant 1¼ cups) double (heavy) cream
80g (2¾oz/⅓ cup) smooth peanut butter
¼ tsp fine sea salt
100g (3½oz) dark chocolate, finely chopped

Add all the ingredients apart from the chocolate to a saucepan. Over a medium heat, bring the sauce to a simmer, stirring frequently. Let it cook for 3–5 minutes until smooth and glossy.

Remove from the heat and stir in the chocolate until melted. Let the sauce cool and thicken a little for 10 minutes, then use straight away, or pour it into a clean jar and store in the fridge.

caramelized cereal crunch

MAKE AHEAD

Make the cereal crunch up to 5 days ahead and store in an airtight container.

Make the plum and vanilla compote up to 3 days ahead and store in an airtight container in the fridge.

This is something on the side that's quite fun and a little bit unexpected. But it brings the best type of sweet, textured crunch. I've tried this with loads of different cereals and they all pretty much work, so it's just a question of what you're after. Unsweetened wheat cereals bring a more grown-up, nutty feel. Or for something more playful, a mix of rice krispies, cornflakes and honey loops works a treat. Use this anywhere you want some major crunch, and get creative with the finishings if you fancy – a dusting of cinnamon or a drizzle of dark chocolate makes things even more interesting.

Makes enough for 8–12 servings

90g (3¼oz/scant ½ cup) caster (superfine) sugar
25ml (1fl oz/1½ Tbsp) water
70g (2½oz) your choice of cereal, lightly crushed
20g (1½ Tbsp) unsalted butter
½ tsp flaky sea salt, plus extra to finish

Line a baking tray with baking paper.

Add the sugar and water to a wide, shallow saucepan and heat gently until melted. Tip in the cereal and stir to coat.

Continue stirring until the sugar looks crystallized. It will look like it's gone wrong, but keep stirring and the sugar will turn dry and sandy.

After about 2–4 minutes, the sugar will begin to melt again and turn a golden colour. Continue stirring to evenly coat the cereal before adding the butter and salt.

Once the cereal is coated and a deep amber colour, remove from the heat and tip it onto the lined baking tray.

Sprinkle a little flaky sea salt on top and let it cool completely and firm up.

Once cool, break the cereal up into smaller pieces and store in an airtight container.

plum & vanilla compote

This is for when you need something a little bit saucy on the side. Whether it's to cut through the creaminess of a slice of burnt Basque cheesecake (page 103), to spoon on top of marzipan yoghurt cakes (page 163) or to layer inside my date night cake (page 87), this is a flexible and forgiving compote that is great to put together quickly when needed. Even the most firm, unripe plums can be transformed into something softened and syrupy that will complement a whole range of desserts.

I like to keep it quite chunky; we're not making a jam so be careful not to overcook the plums.

Makes about 350ml (12fl oz/1½ cups)

300g (10½oz) plums (ideally ripe)
60g (2¼oz/5 Tbsp) caster (superfine) sugar
2 Tbsp water
1 Tbsp lemon juice
1 vanilla pod (bean)

Slice the plums in half and remove the stone (pit). Cut into quarters and place in a pan along with the sugar, water and lemon juice.

Use a sharp knife to split the vanilla pod open down the middle and scrape out the seeds. Add the pod and seeds to the pan.

Simmer the plums over a medium heat for 8–10 minutes, stirring occasionally. You can use the back of a spoon to break them down into smaller chunks. Once the plums have softened and look syrupy, remove from the heat and set aside to cool completely.

Transfer the compote to a sterilized jar or airtight container and store in the fridge until needed.

tuiles

I avoided making tuiles for the longest time. They always felt very technical and far too fancy, but after making a dessert that was crying out for a little crunch, I tried making a batch and was surprised at how easy they were. And they're ideal to make when you've got a bit of leftover egg white, as I so often do. I prefer making tuiles as one large piece that just needs to be broken into shards once cool, as opposed to individual biscuits which, although pretty, are much more faffy.

Keep an eye on them, as they brown very quickly, but once you've made them a couple of times, you'll get the hang of it.

Serves 6–8

35g (1¼oz/2½ Tbsp) unsalted butter, softened
35g (1¼oz/4 Tbsp) icing (confectioners') sugar
¼ tsp fine sea salt
40g (1½oz) egg white (about 1 large egg)
45g (1⅔oz/5½ Tbsp) plain (all-purpose) flour
handful of flaked (slivered) almonds (optional)

Preheat the oven to 180°C (160°C fan/ 350°F/gas mark 4). Line a large baking tray with baking paper.

Add the butter, icing sugar and salt to a small bowl and beat with a spatula until smooth. Mix in the egg white, followed by the flour.

Mix well until you have a smooth batter. Spoon the batter onto the baking sheet (you can use a few dabs of the batter to help stick the baking paper down to the tray) and spread it thinly and evenly, so it is about 1–2mm (1⁄16in) thick.

Top with flaked almonds, if using, and bake for 8–10 minutes until the tuile is dry to the touch and comes away from the paper easily.

Remove from the oven and let cool completely. It will firm up as it cools. Break into shards and serve with your chosen dessert.

MAKE AHEAD

Make up to 4 days ahead and store in an airtight container.

infused caramel sauce

MAKE AHEAD

Make the caramel sauce up to 5 days in advance and store in a jar or airtight container in the fridge.

Make the sesame crunch up to 3 days ahead and store in an airtight container.

I use caramel sauces all the time. They're incredibly versatile and you can make them days in advance, meaning you have one less thing to do. Infusing your caramel sauce opens up possibilities and can gently transform a dessert into something new each time. My go-to is usually fresh herbs, anything from sage to thyme and rosemary. But you can infuse a whole range of things – tea, coffee beans, spices, toasted nuts or coconut, and plenty more. Have a play around with quantities until you get the right amount of infusion to your taste.

Makes 1 x 350ml (12fl oz/1½ cups) jar

150ml (5fl oz/scant ⅔ cup) double (heavy) cream
a few fresh herb sprigs, or 1 Tbsp coffee beans, or 2–3 tea bags, or your flavouring of choice (see introduction)
200g (7oz/1 cup) caster (superfine) sugar
40g (1½oz/3 Tbsp) unsalted butter
big pinch of flaky sea salt

Add the cream to a saucepan and heat gently until hot, but don't let it come to the boil. Add in your chosen ingredient to infuse, and remove from the heat. Cover and let the cream cool and infuse for at least 30 minutes, but ideally an hour.

Strain the cream through a sieve (strainer) and pour it back into the pan, discarding any solids. Reheat gently until warmed through, and set aside.

In a separate clean pan, add the sugar and heat gently until it starts to melt. Give the pan a swirl every so often to help it melt evenly. Once the sugar turns a deep amber colour, add in the butter and whisk quickly to combine. The caramel will bubble up and spatter, so be careful!

Slowly pour in the warmed cream, while whisking. Again, the caramel will bubble up. Let the caramel cook for another 30 seconds before removing from the heat and stirring in the salt. Let it cool completely before using.

sesame crunch

These remind me of sesame snaps, with their nutty taste and toasty and caramelized seeds. They are moreishly addictive and far too easy to mindlessly snack on, but they make a great topping for ice creams, trifles and tarts.

This makes a generous batch so make sure to liberally sprinkle it on top of anything and everything.

Makes 1 x 200ml (7fl oz/scant 1 cup) jar

70g (2½oz/generous ⅓ cup) caster (superfine) sugar
60ml (2fl oz/¼ cup) water
80g (2¾oz/generous ½ cup) sesame seeds
flaky sea salt

Line a baking tray with baking paper.

Put the sugar, water and sesame seeds in a small saucepan. Bring to the boil and stir frequently before reducing the heat to low and letting the water evaporate.

The seeds will look dry and sandy. Continue to cook and stir until the sugar starts to melt and turn golden brown. The seeds will start clumping together and get coated in the caramelized sugar.

Remove from the heat and tip the mixture onto the lined tray. Sprinkle with a little flaky sea salt and leave to cool completely before using.

index

acknowledgements

This is my third(!) cookbook and I'm always asked if it gets any easier each time round. I guess, the third time round, I know what to expect and I can mentally prepare for the long recipe testing days, the endless washing up and the multiple failed attempts to get a recipe just right. But it still requires so much of you creatively and it's not something you can do alone. So I'm extremely grateful for all the people involved in bringing this book to life and making the whole process so much more fun.

To you, the readers who have bought a copy. Sending you the biggest thank you for your continued support! Seeing pictures of what you've made and reading all of your messages puts the biggest smile on my face. I truly hope the recipes inspire you, and are enjoyed by whoever is round the table with you.

To the team at Quadrille, thank you for working with me on another beautiful book and seeing the vision of what I wanted to create. Thank you to Stacey for being such a thoughtful and kind editor. And to Katherine for being so patient with all my back and forth on the book design.

To Laura, the woman behind the lens! Truly the best in the biz. Shoot days can be long and tiring but I always look forward to being in your studio and starting the day with a coffee and catch up. Thank you for all the stunning images and for encouraging my Worldle habit.

To Jo, thank you for your infectious enthusiasm on the shoots and for reminding me to stretch.

Thank you Matt for all your retouching skills, especially with the braids!

To Anna, it's always such a joy to work with you. You have the best taste in plates, bowls and gingham tablecloths. Thank you for loving everything I make and inspiring me to pour chocolate custard on my rice pudding. Genius.

To Julia, thank you for being such a helpful and calming presence on shoot days. I know my recipes are in safe hands when you're there. To Alice and Lucy, thank you for all your help in the kitchen – you both made my job a million times easier.

To my sweet friends and family who were able to come to the shoots, it was so fun having you there and being part of the process. I appreciate all of you so much! Thank you for eating it all and for the 10/10 hand modelling.

Thank you to the team at Northbank for the continued support across all my projects.

To my mum, thank you for putting up with yet another book being developed in your kitchen and everywhere being turned upside down. You're the best!

All my love,
Benjamina

Thank you to Aaron Probyn (aaronprobyn.com) for the plates for the Spiced pineapple tart with bay cream (page 37).

Thank you to Victoria and Steve Lemmon for letting us shoot in your beautiful home.

Publishing Director: Sarah Lavelle

Commissioning Editors: Harriet Webster and Stacey Cleworth

Design Manager: Katherine Case

Photographer: Laura Edwards

Food Stylist: Benjamina Ebuehi

Food Stylist Assistants: Julia Aden, Alice Hughes and Lucy Cottle

Prop Stylist: Anna Wilkins

Head of Production: Stephen Lang

Senior Production Controller: Sabeena Atchia

Published in 2024 by Quadrille, an imprint of Hardie Grant Publishing

Quadrille
52–54 Southwark Street
London SE1 1UN
quadrille.com

Cataloguing in Publication Data: a catalogue record for this book is available from the British Library.

ISBN 978 1 83783 039 8

Printed in China

MIX
Paper | Supporting responsible forestry
FSC
www.fsc.org
FSC™ C020056